Gratitude

I would like to express my sincere gratitude for purchasing my coloring book. It is an immense honor to know that you chose to dedicate your time and appreciate my work. I hope each page brings joy, inspiration, and moments of creativity into your life.

Your support means a lot to me and is the fuel that motivates me to continue creating. Thank you for investing in my work and for being part of this colorful journey!

With gratitude,

Silvano dos Santos

Silvano dos Santos
2024

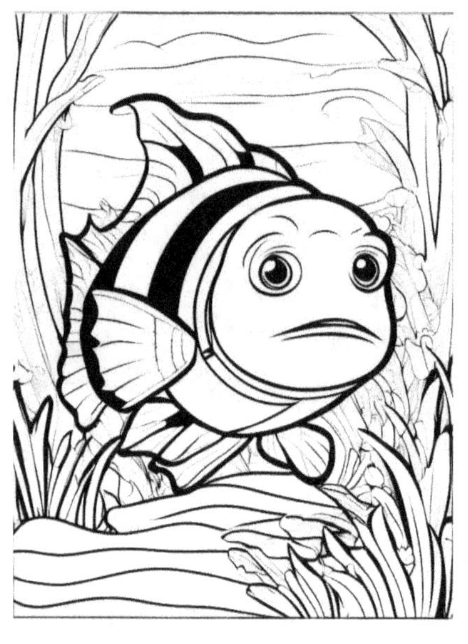
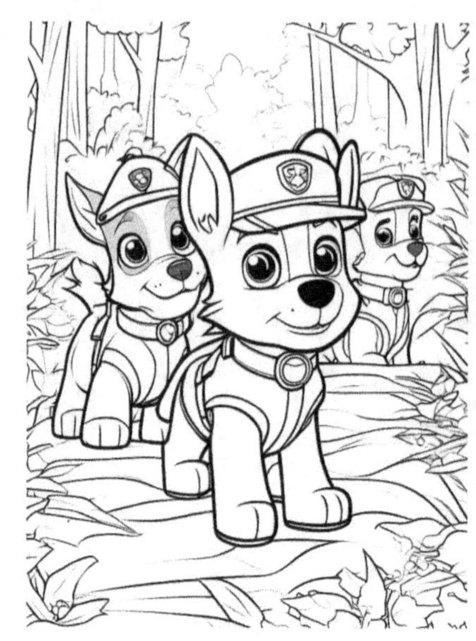

This Book Belongs to:

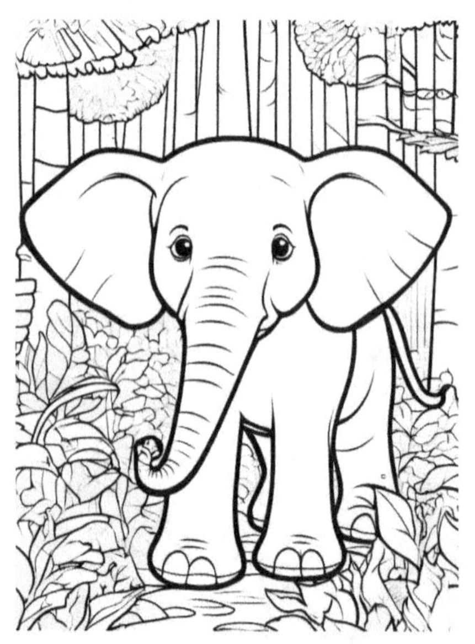
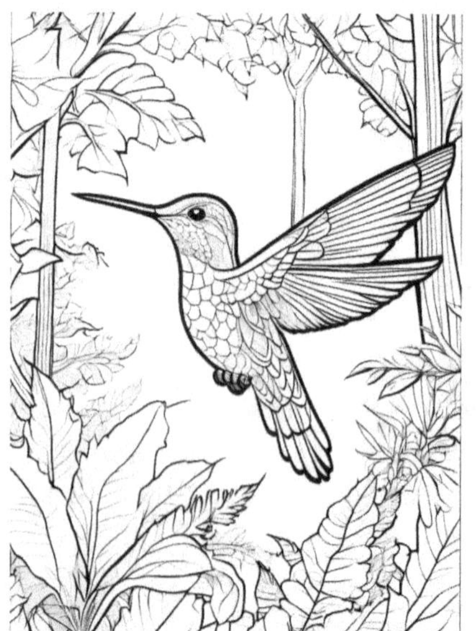

Test Color Page

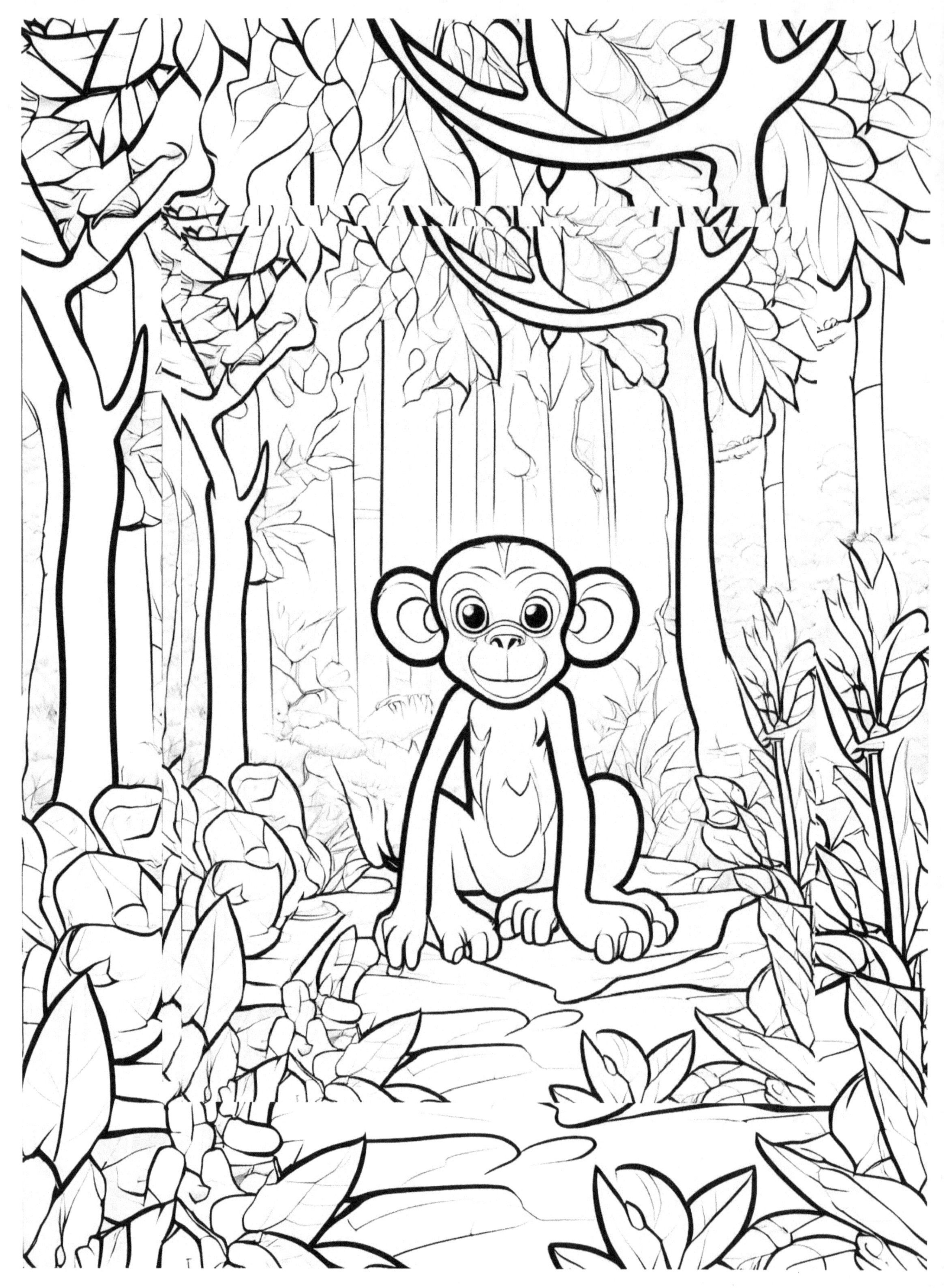

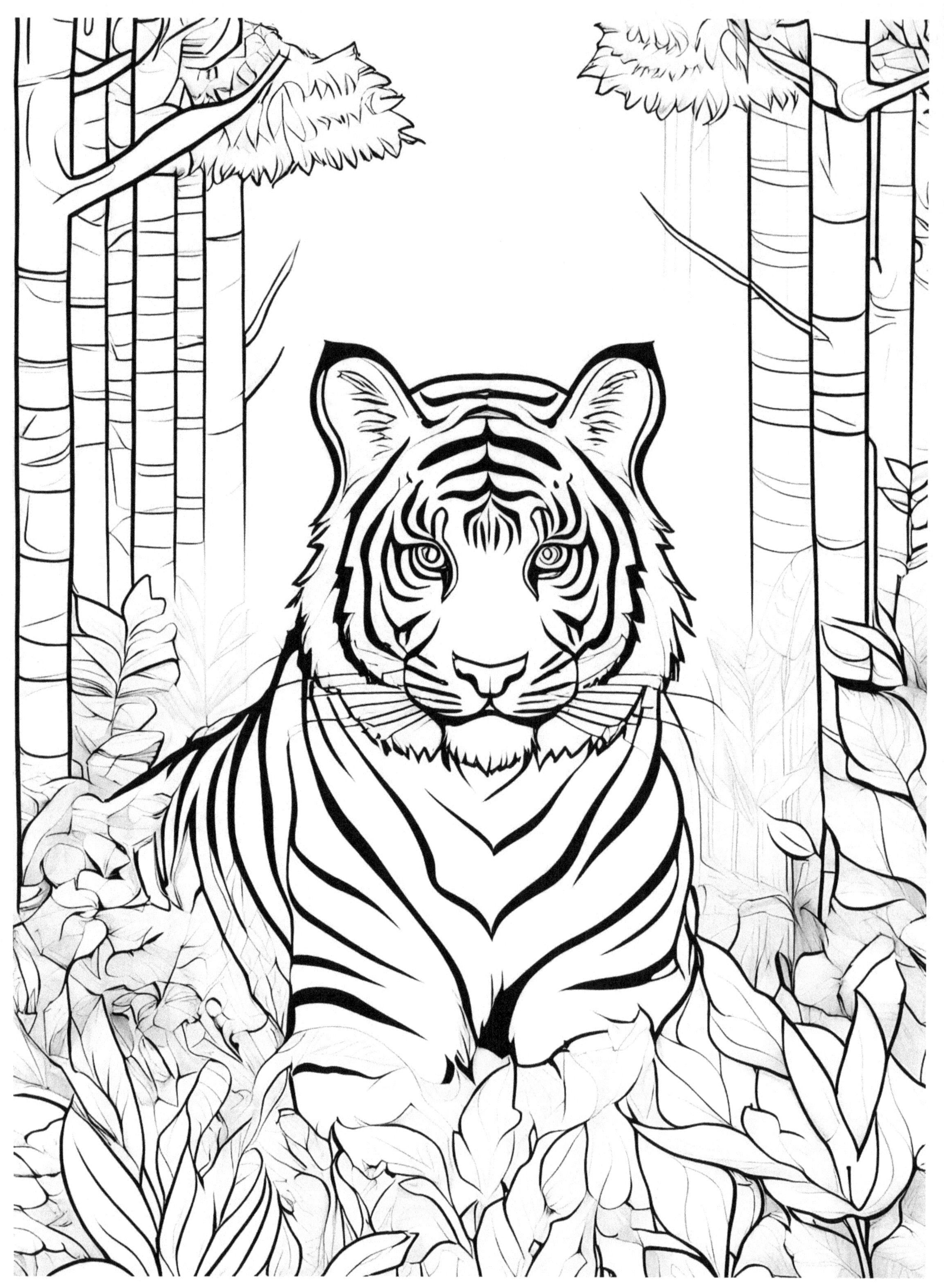

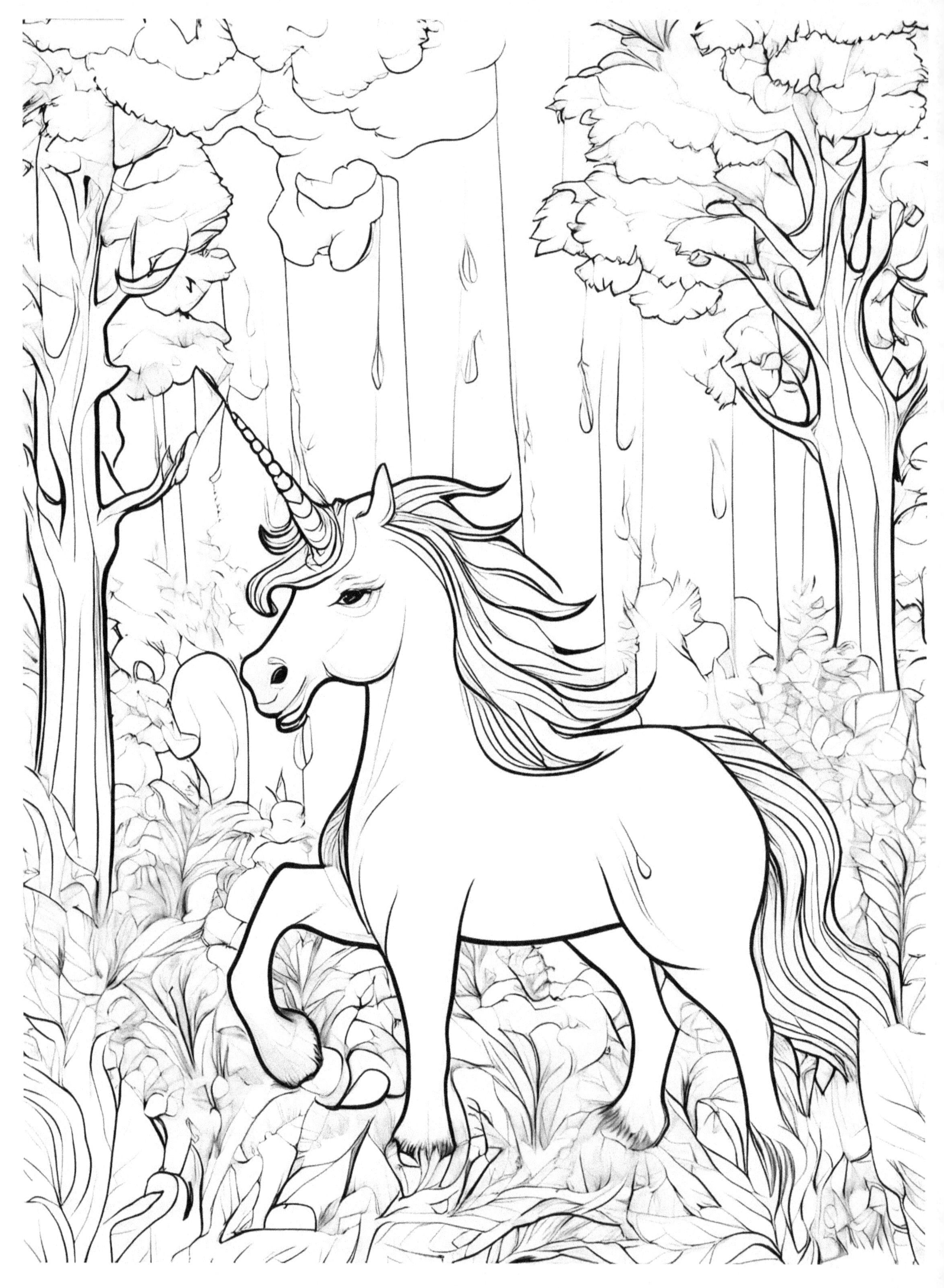

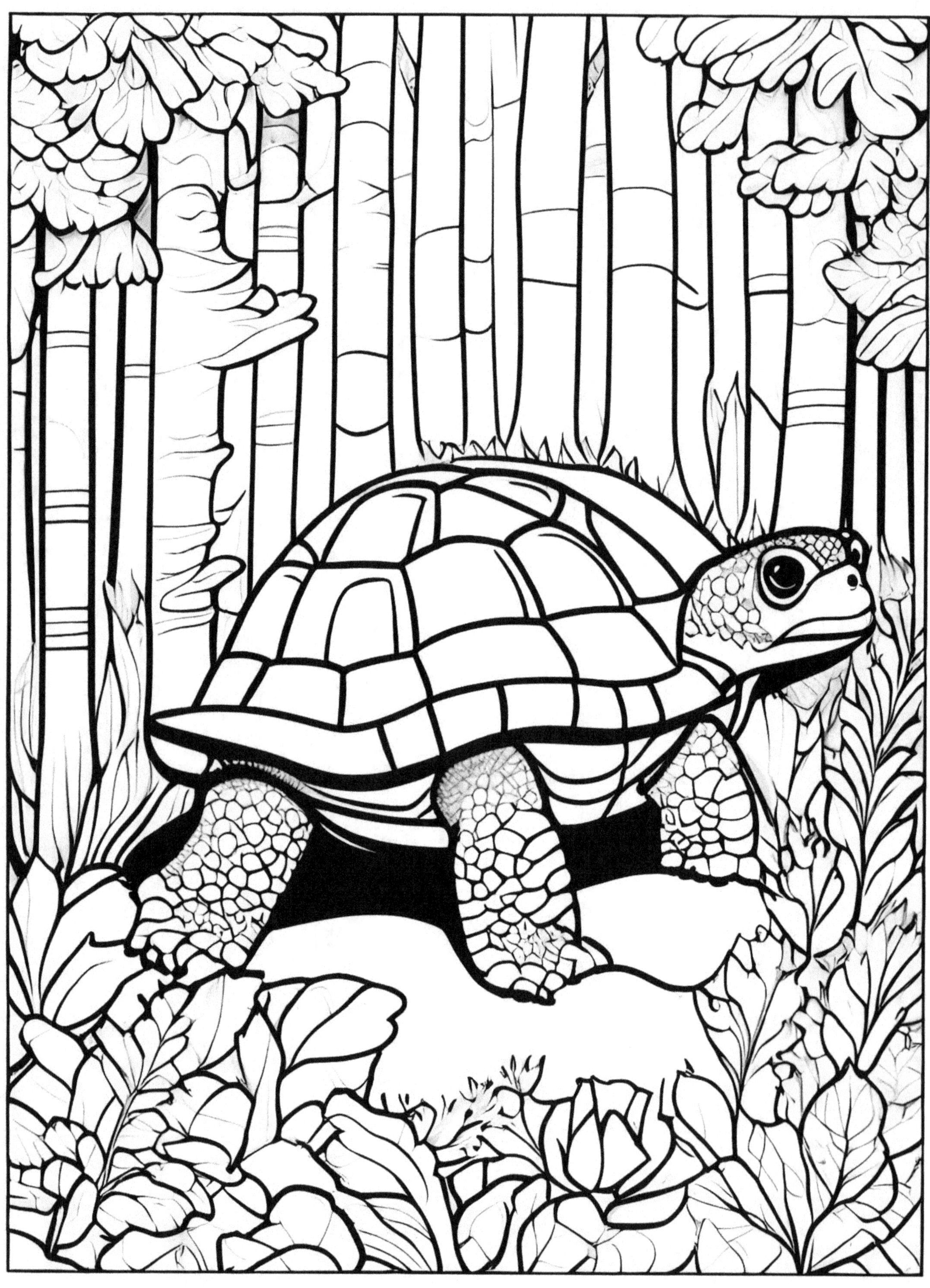

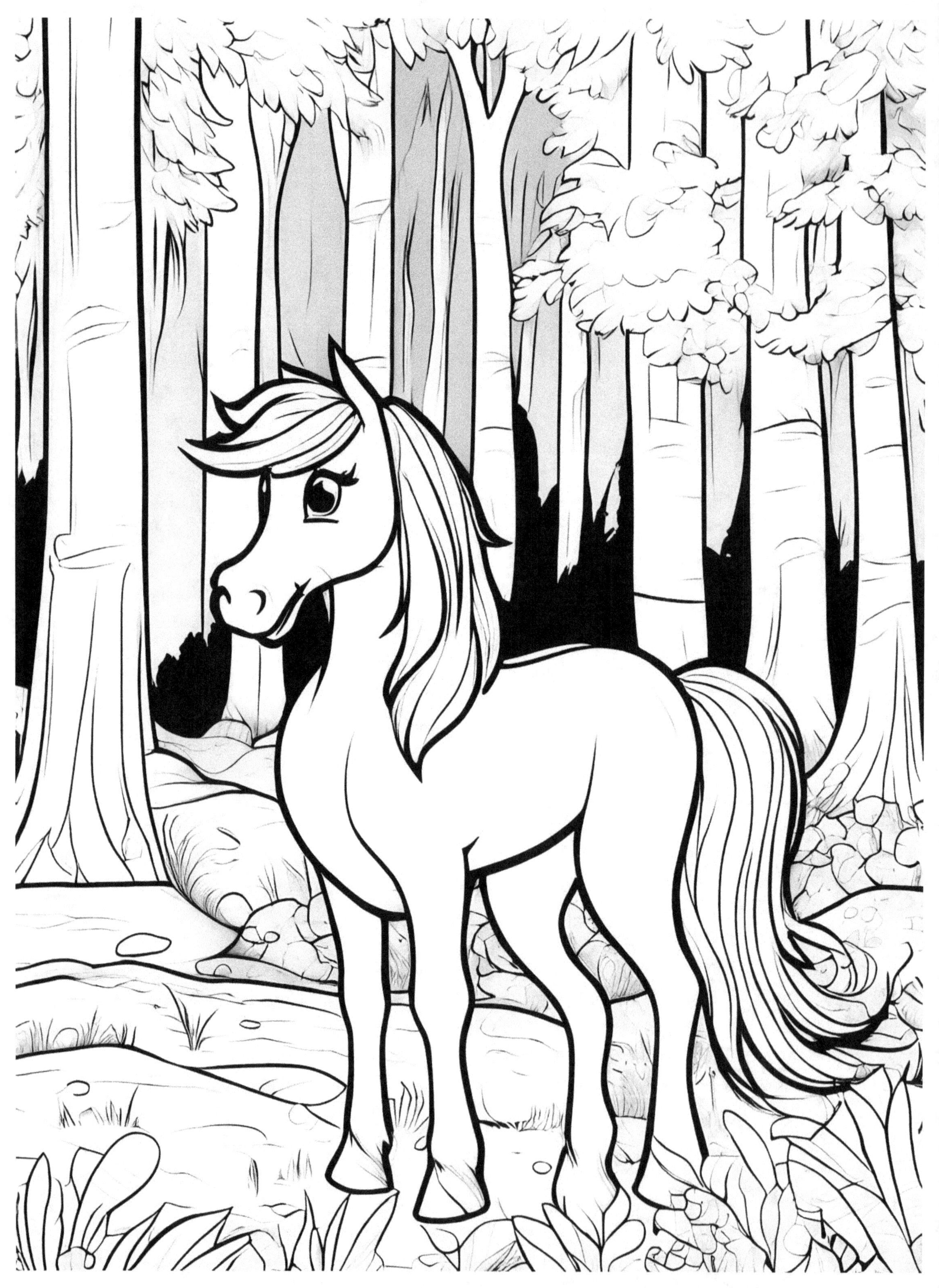

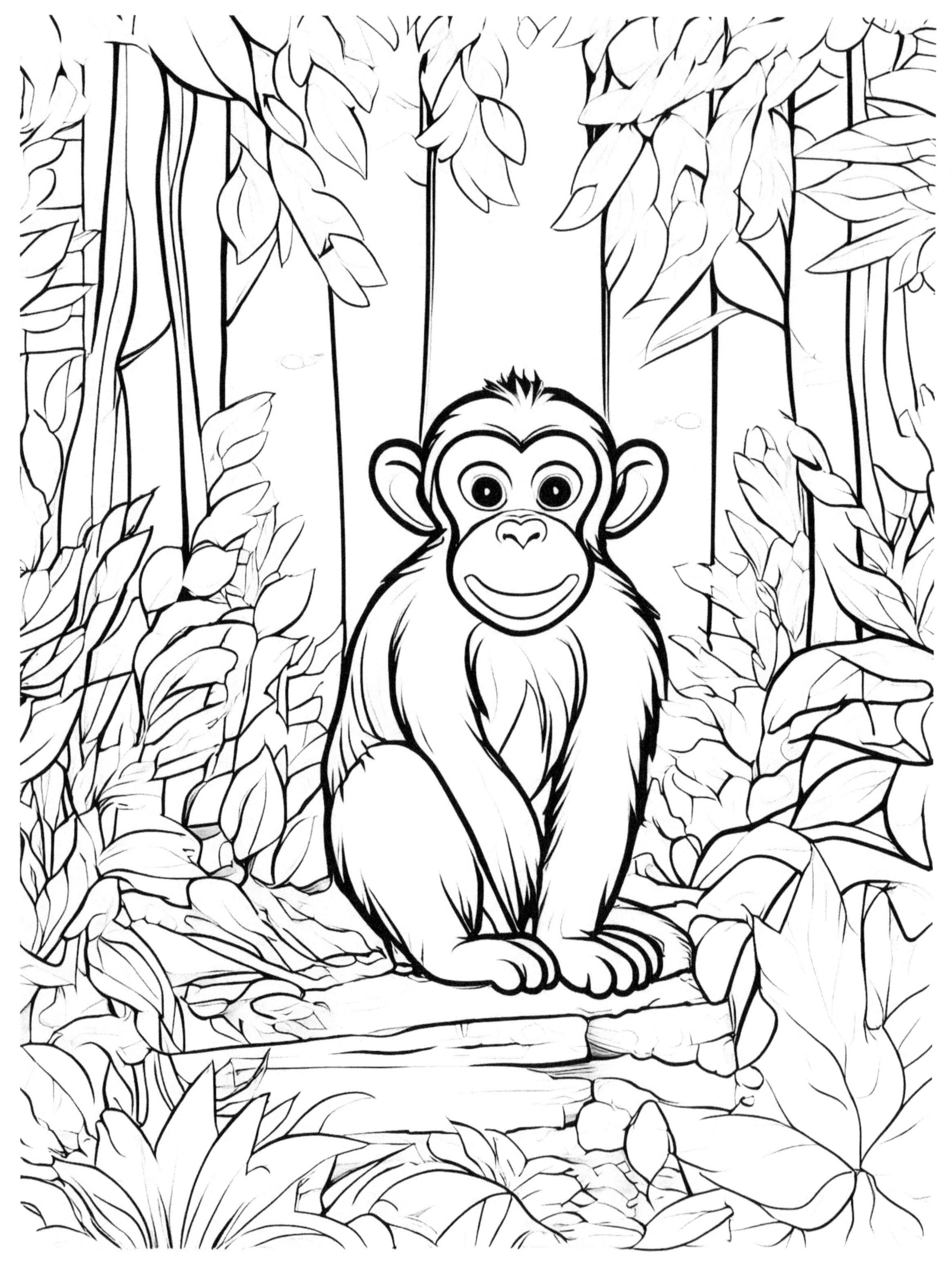

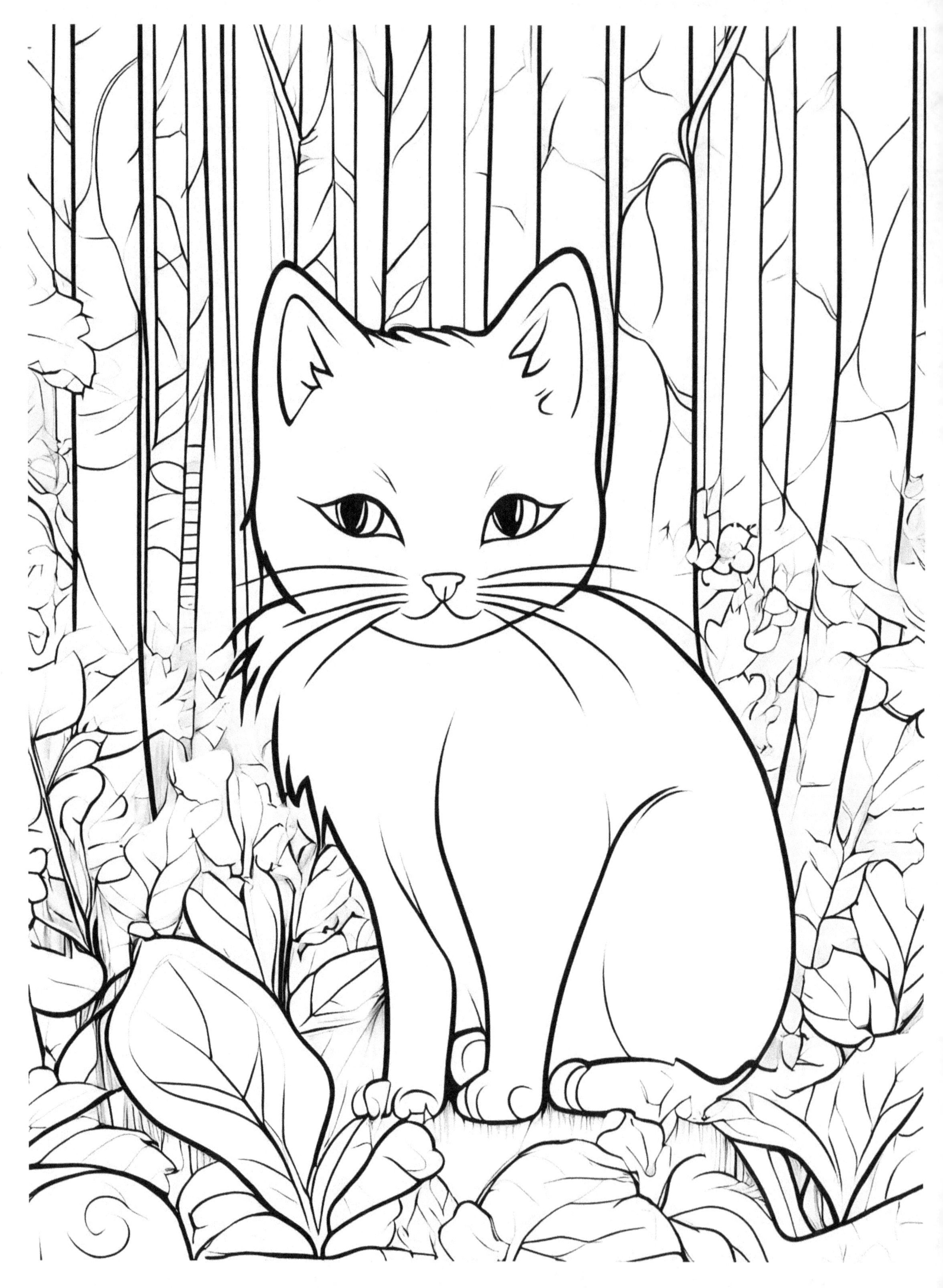

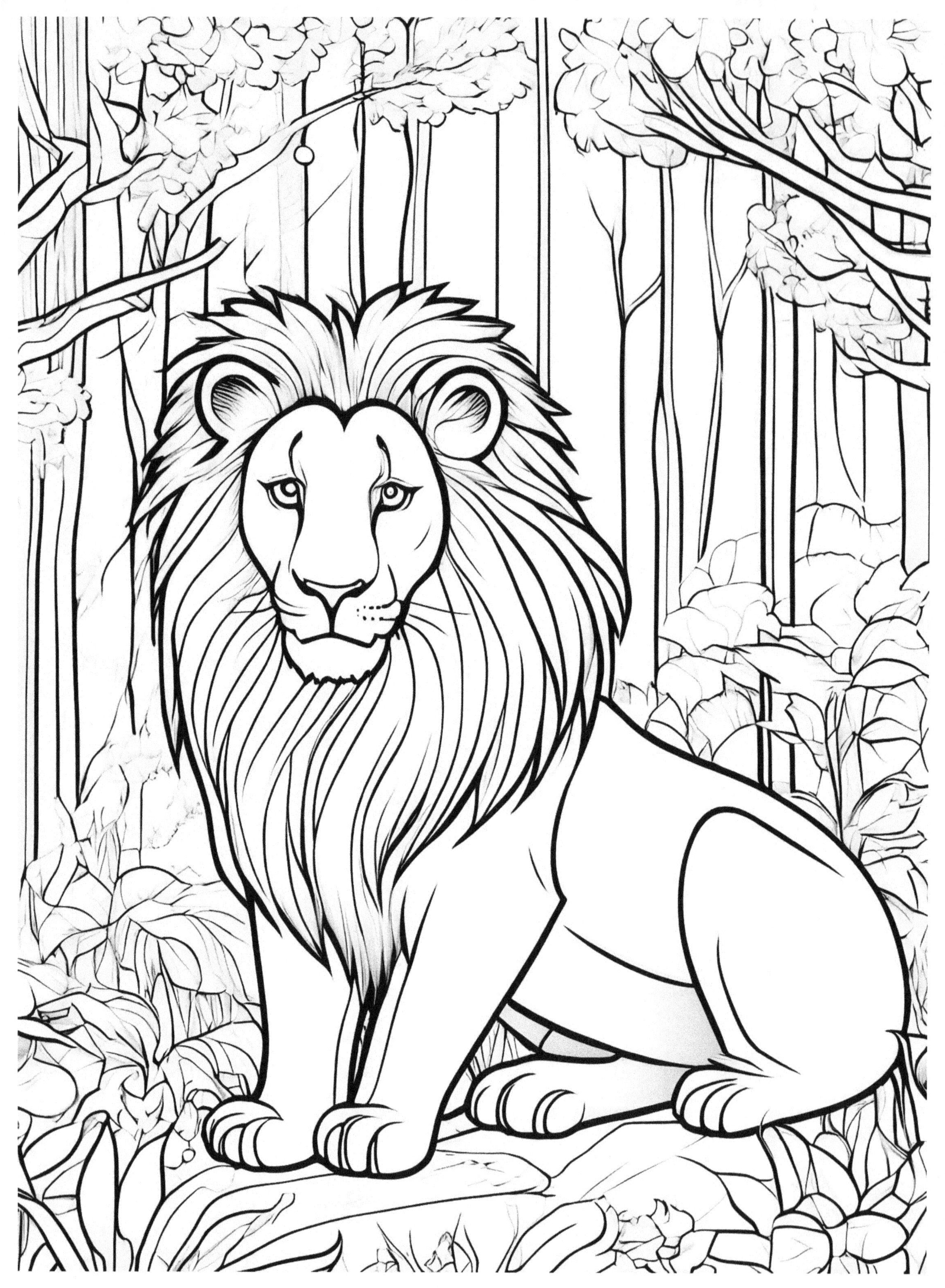

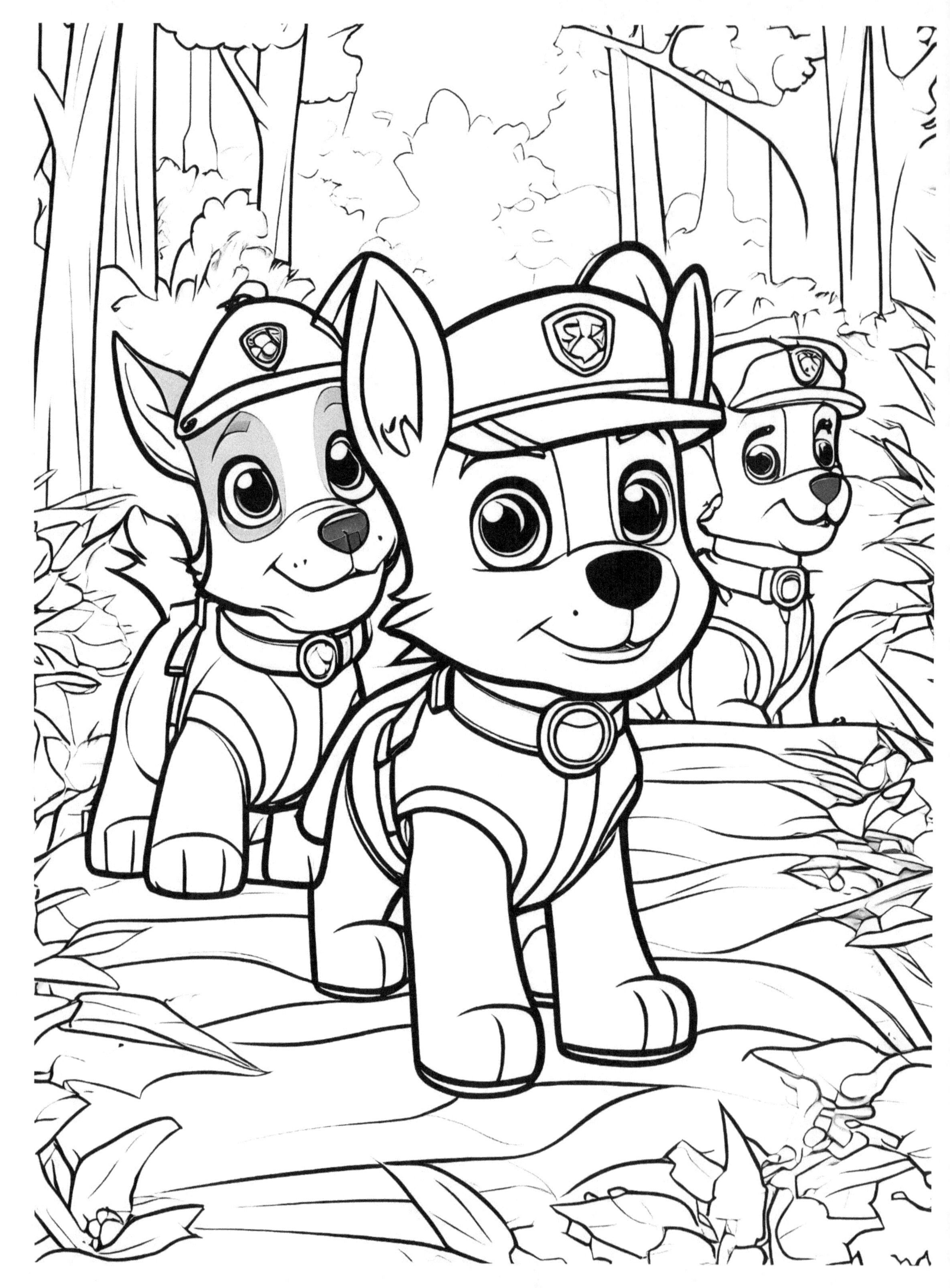

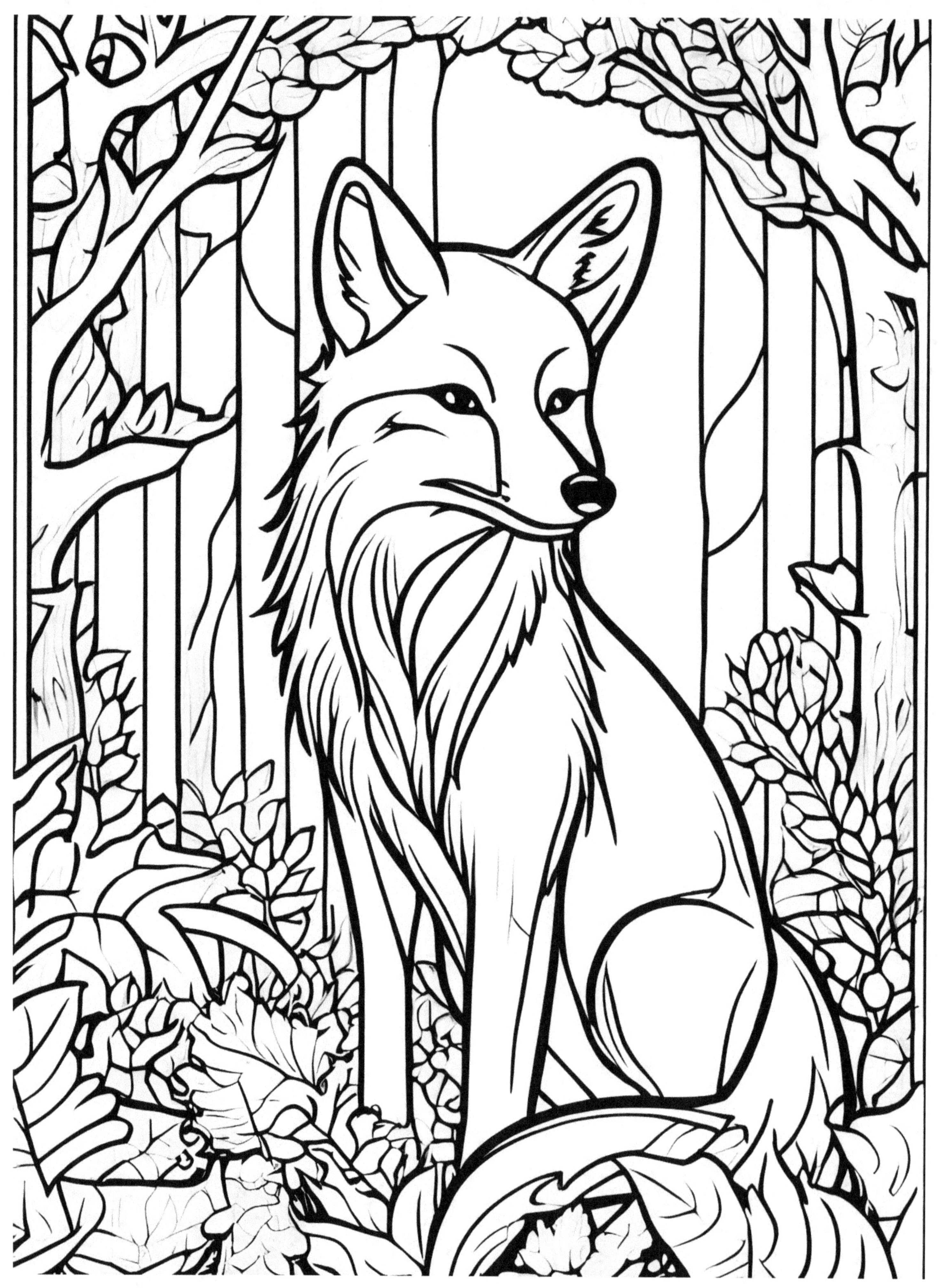

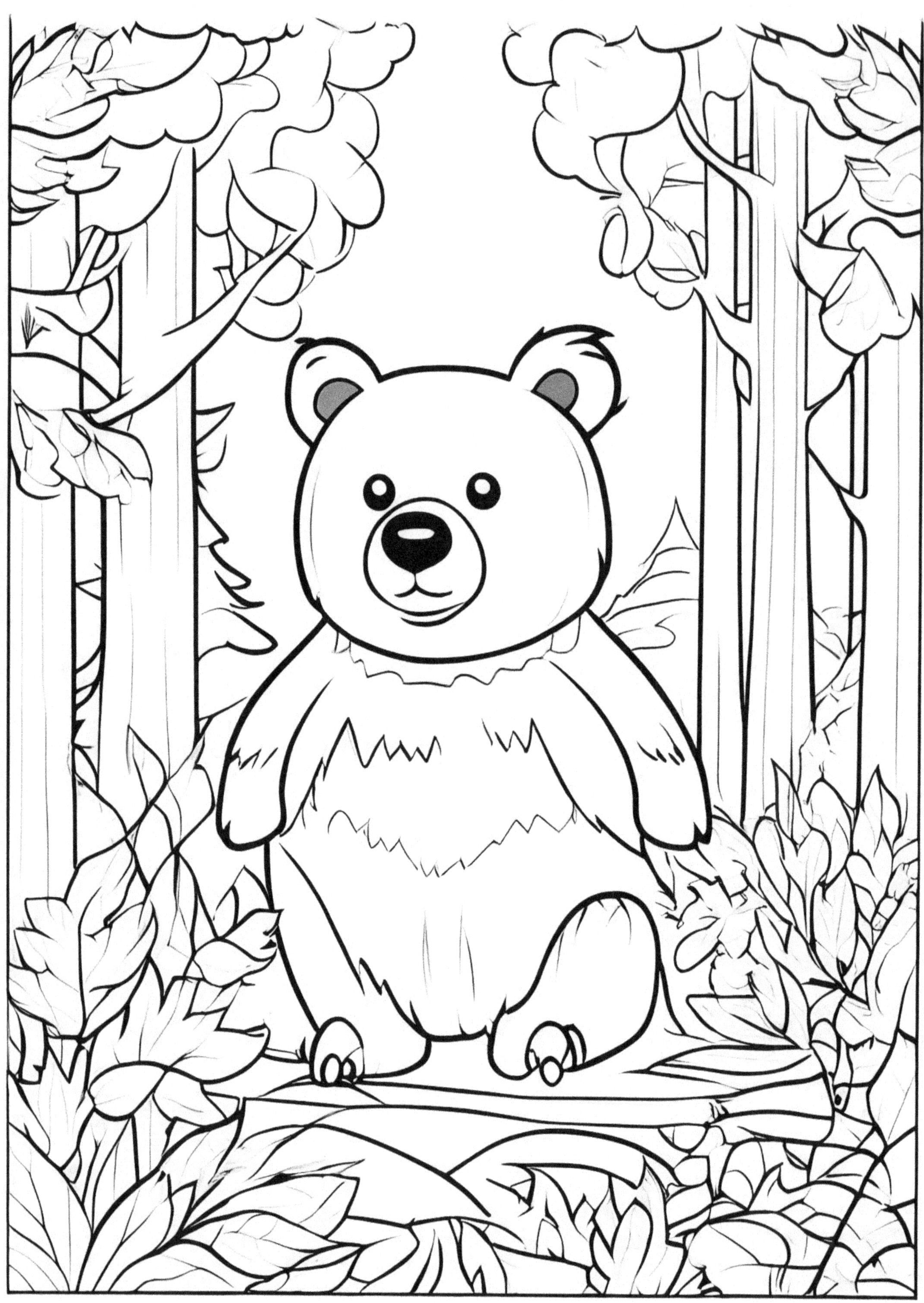

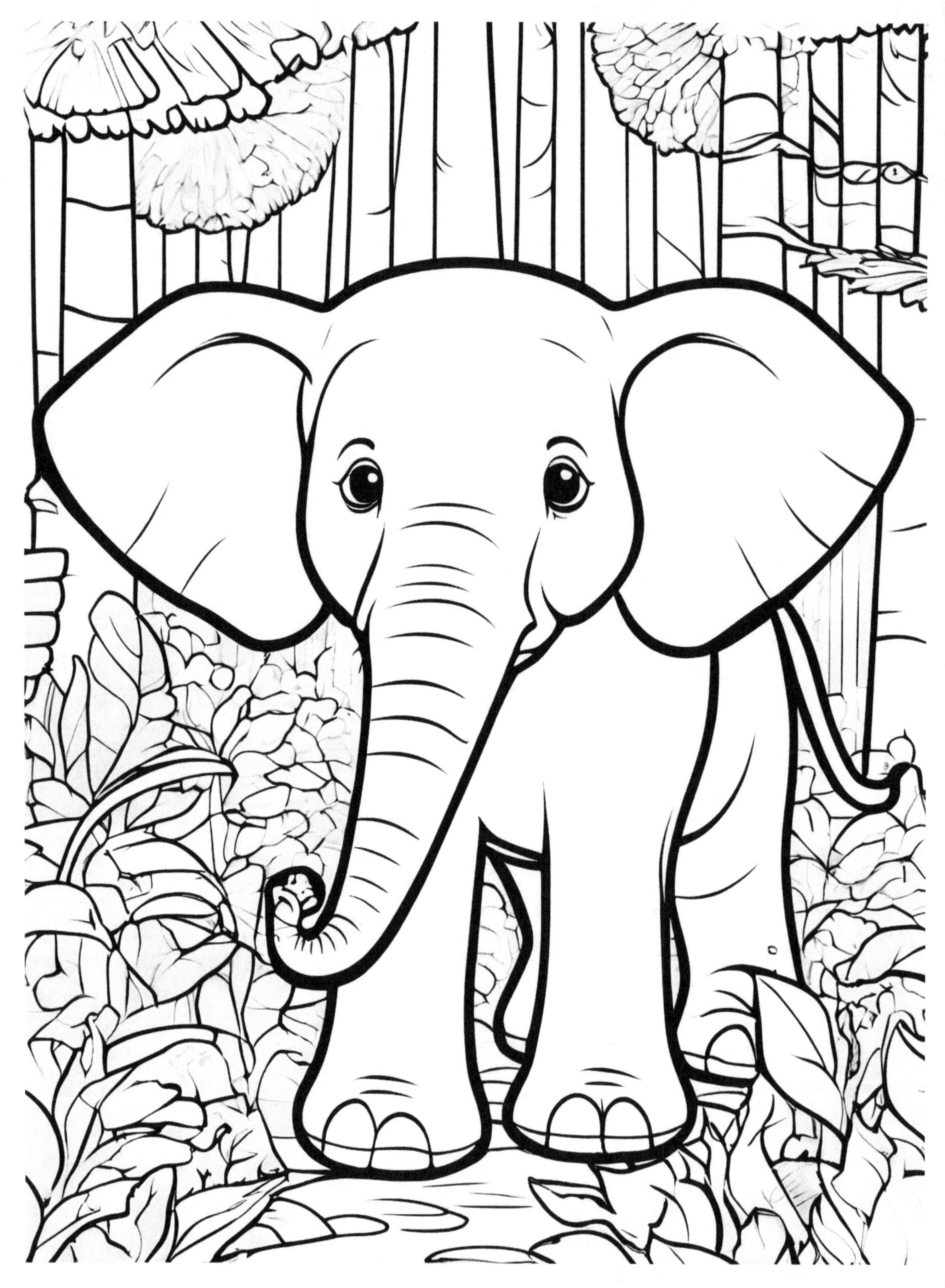

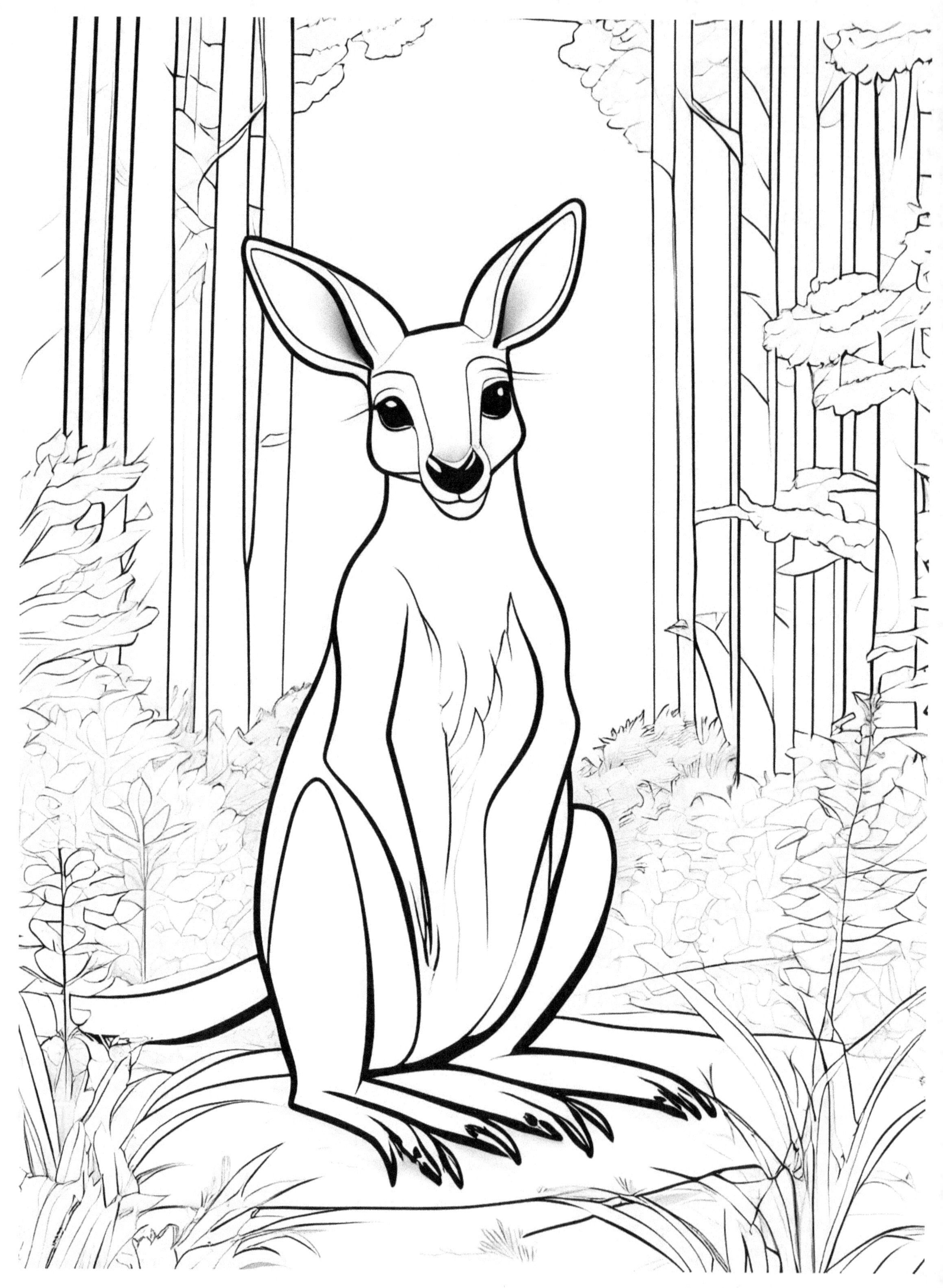

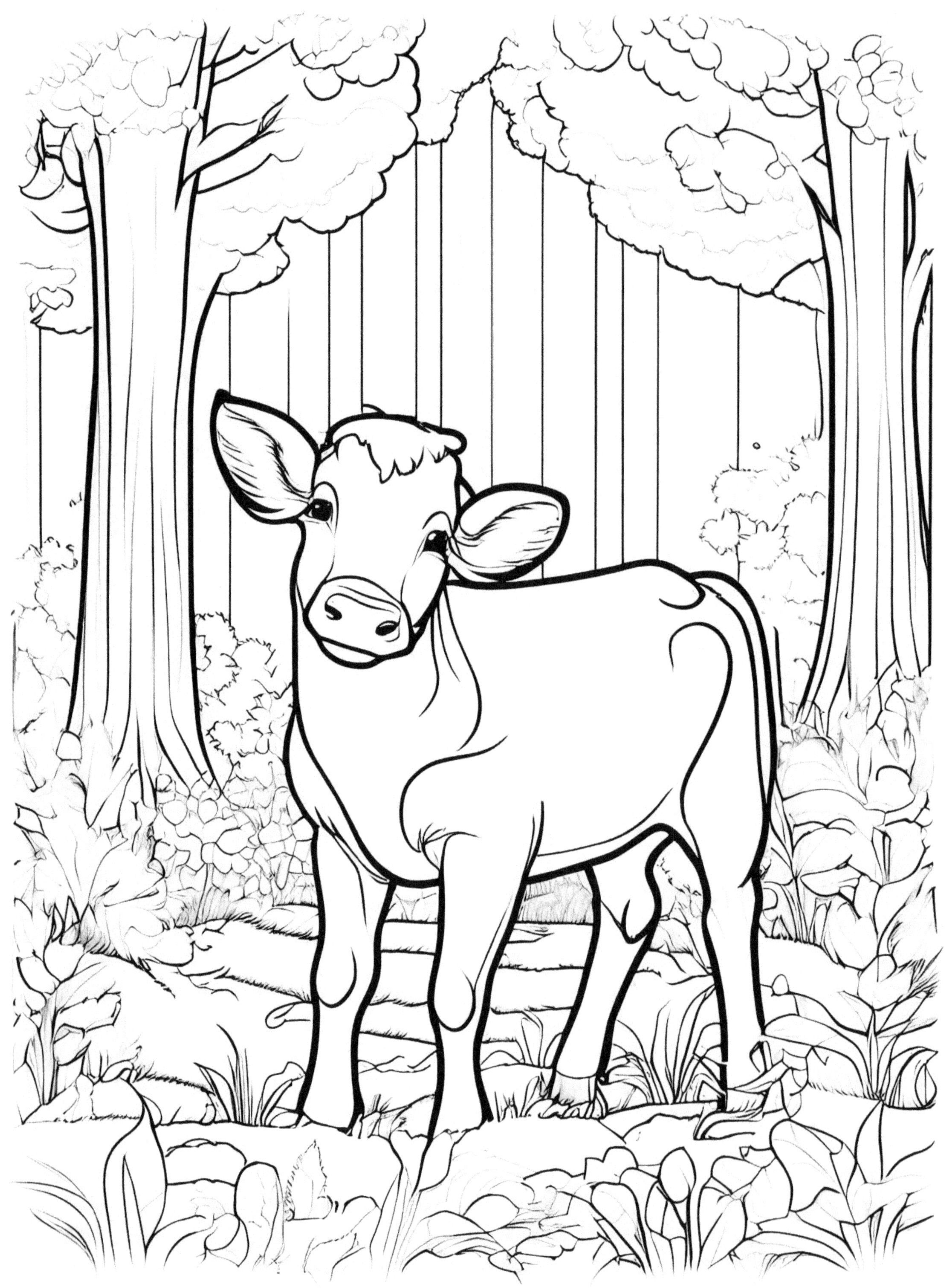

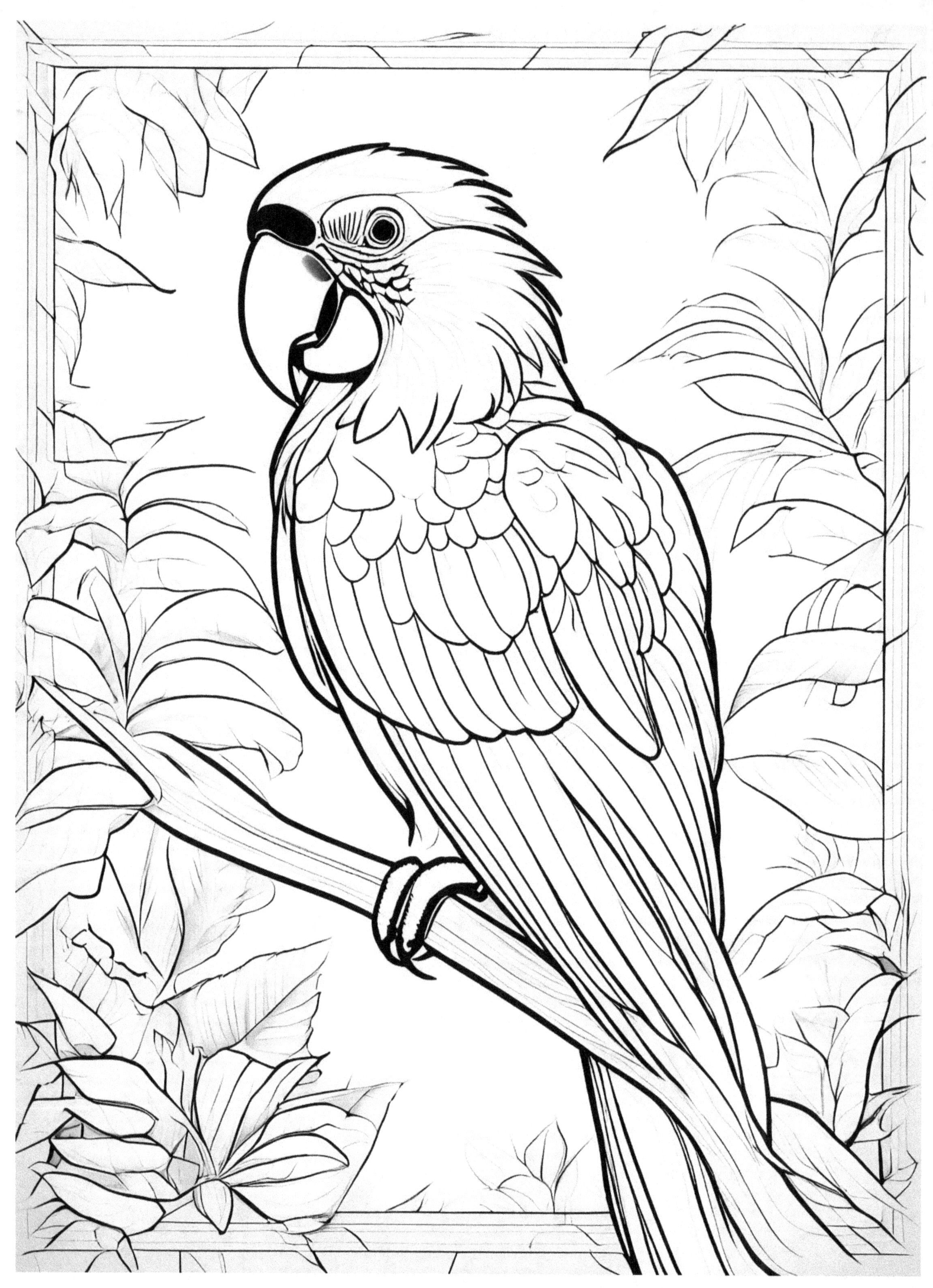

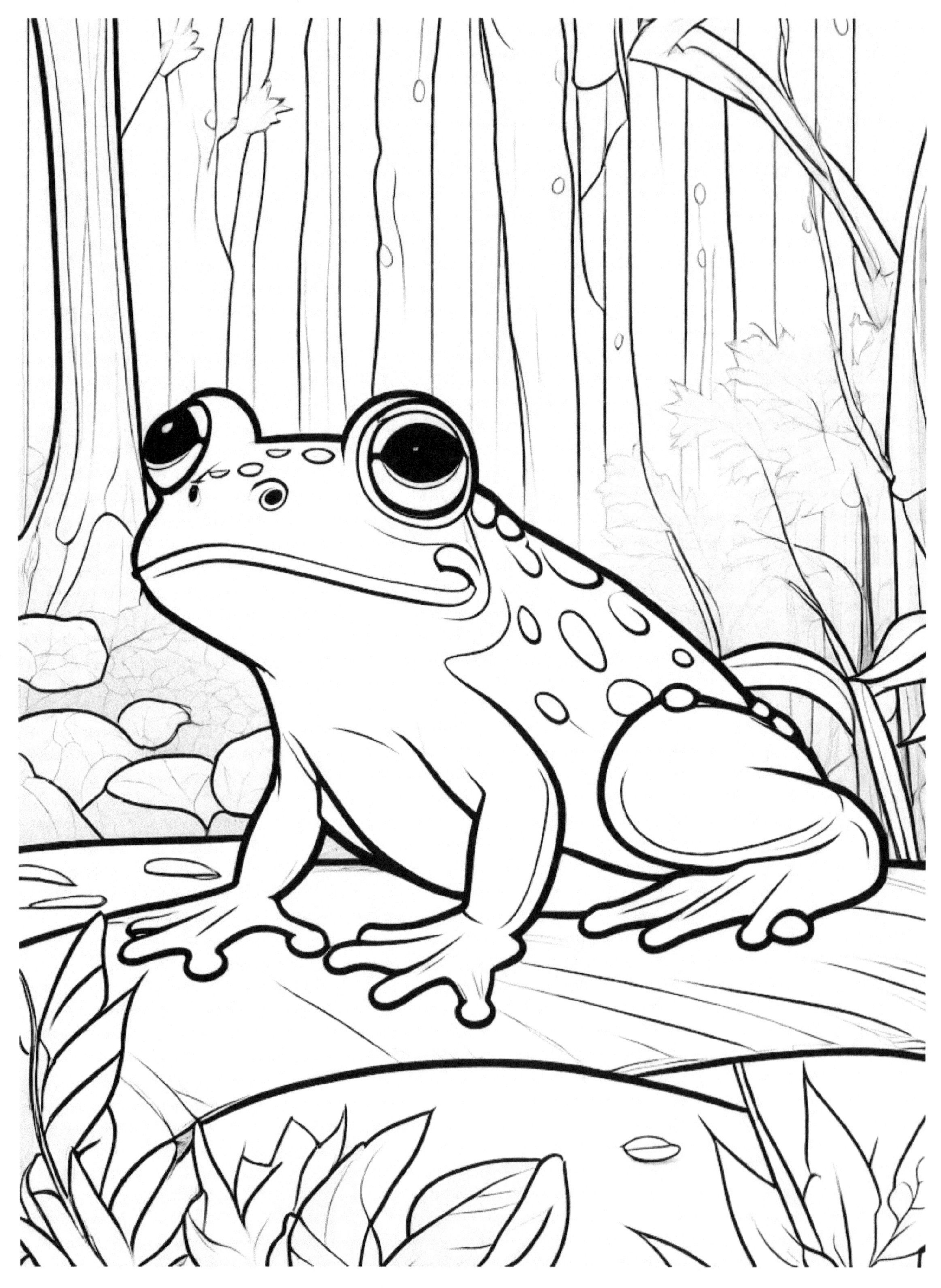

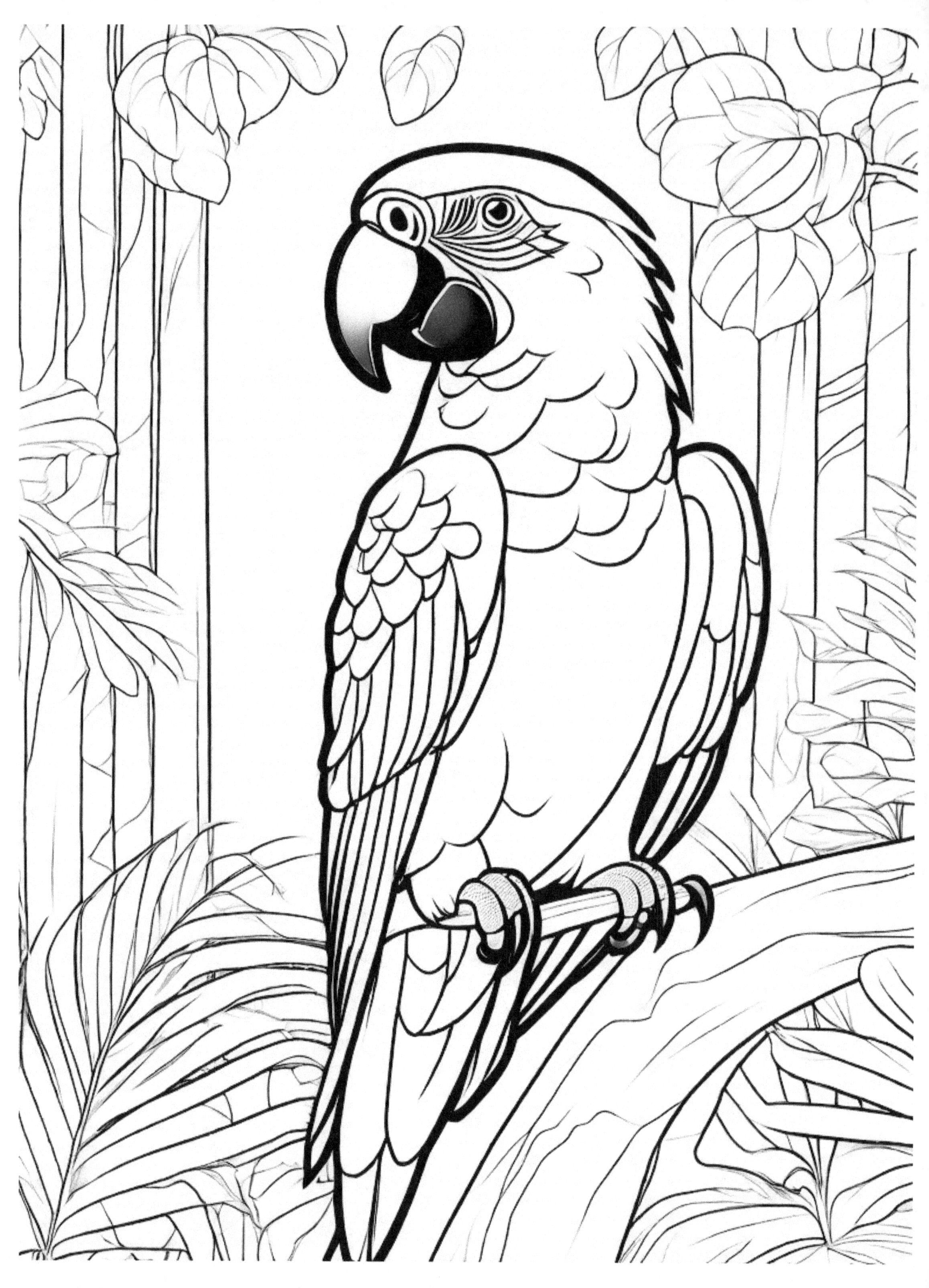

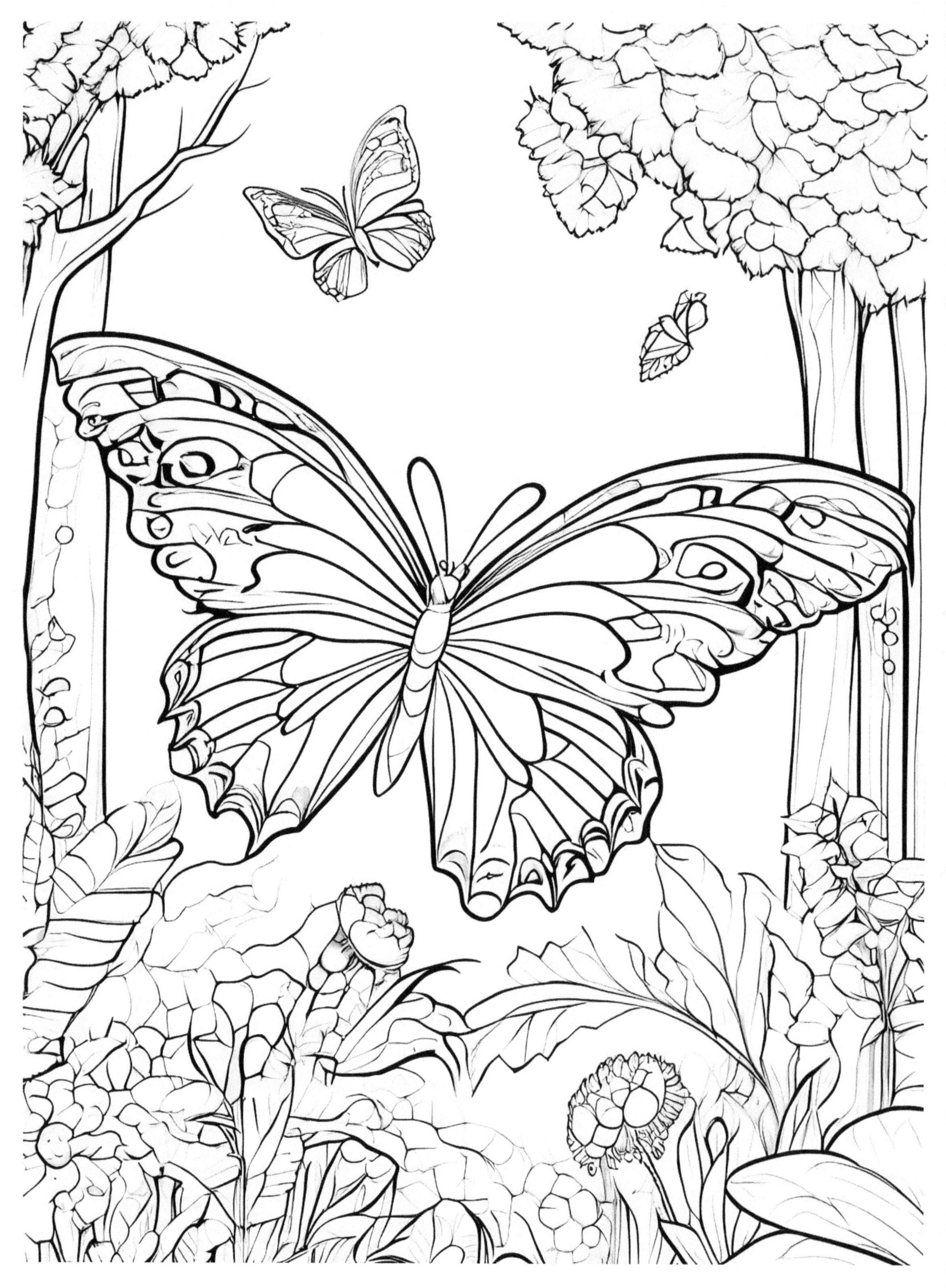

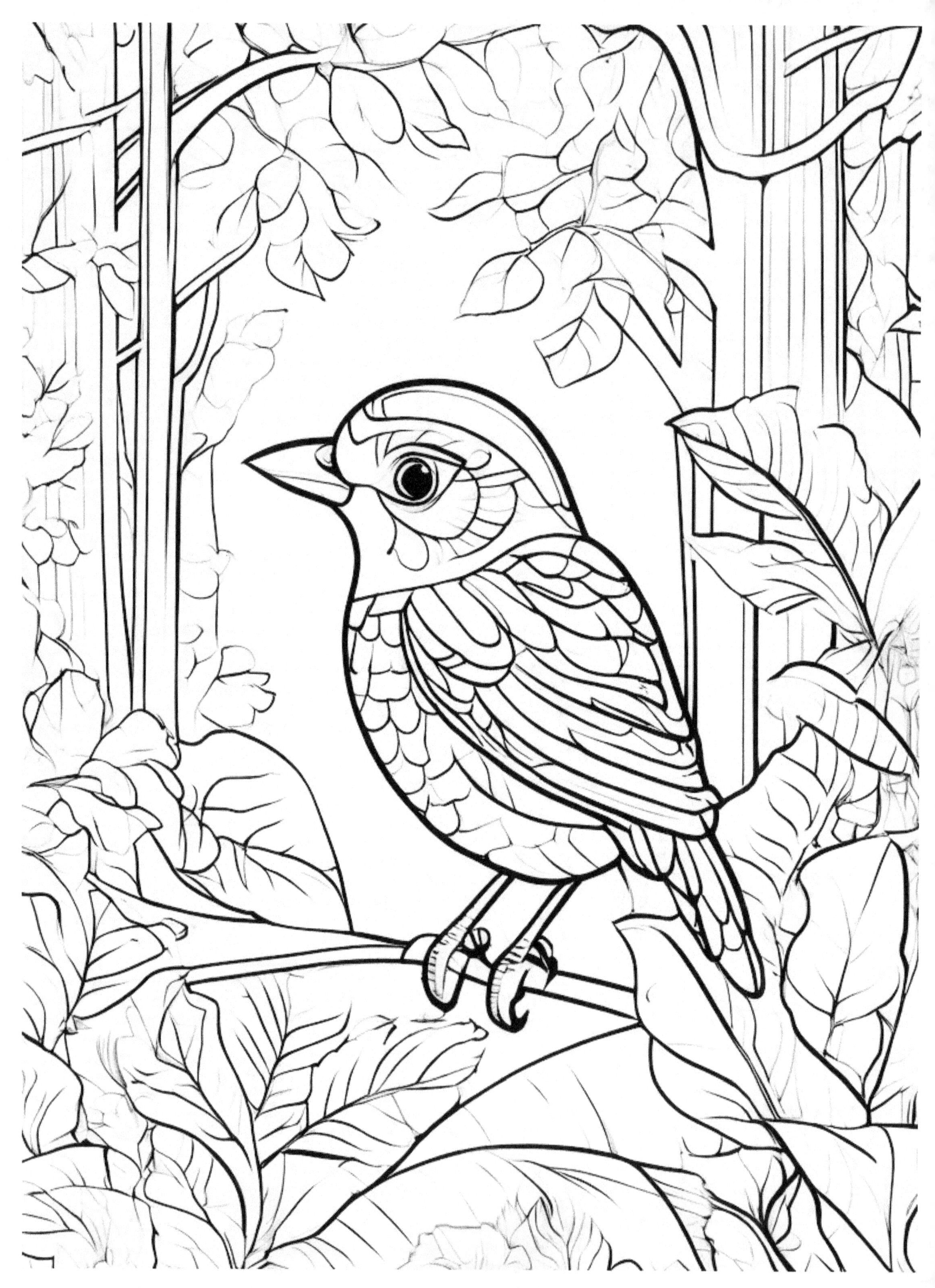

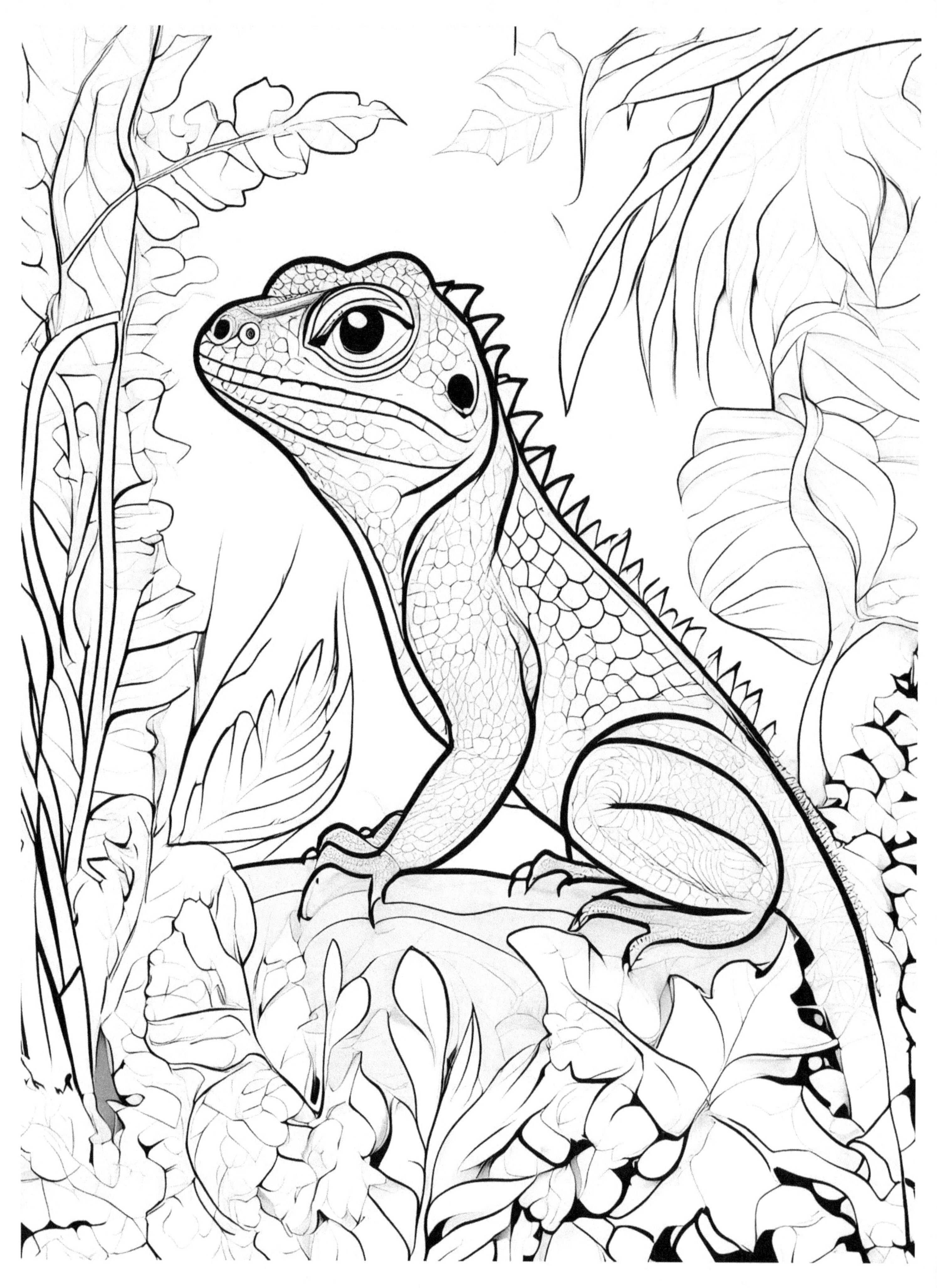

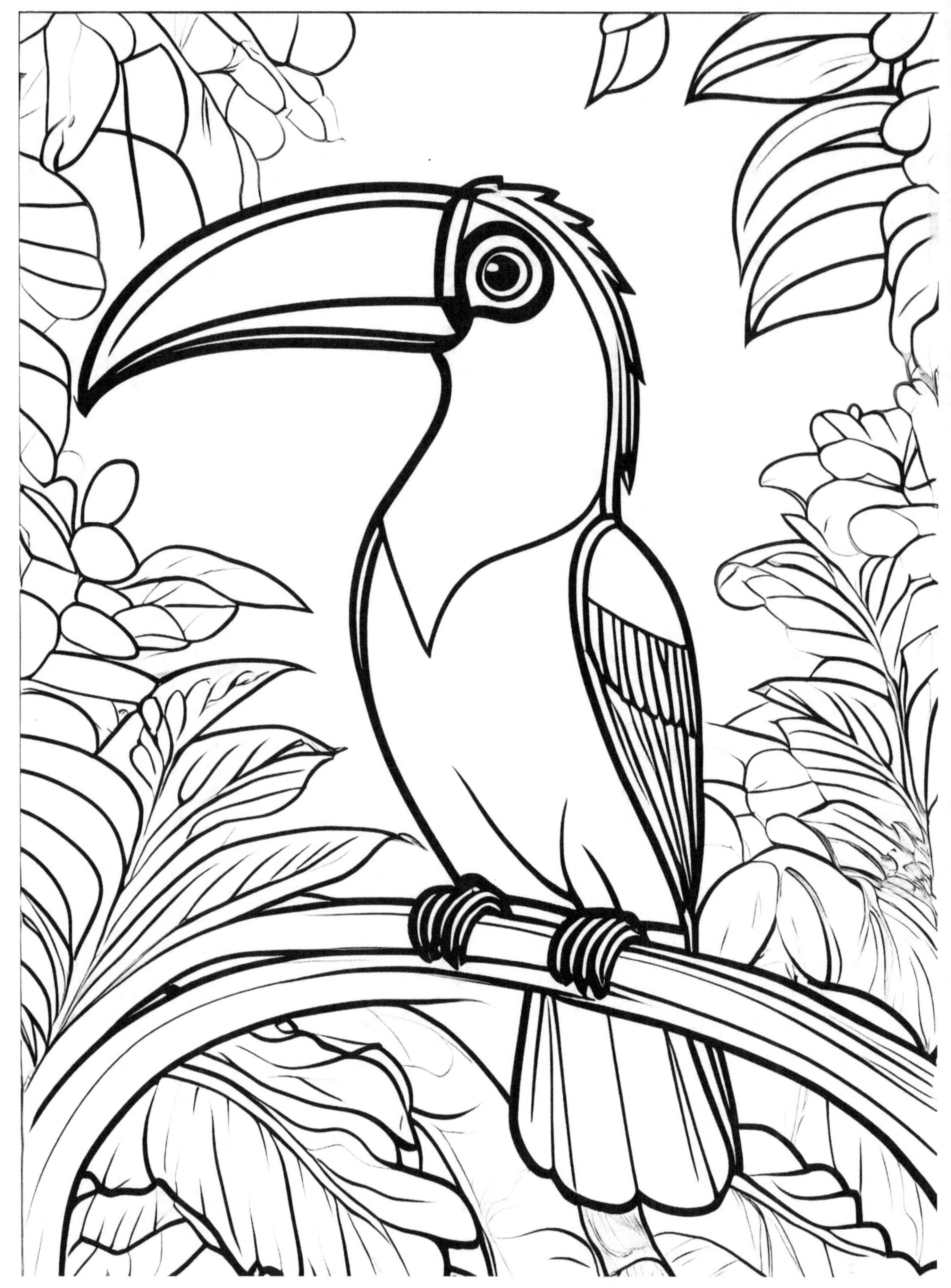

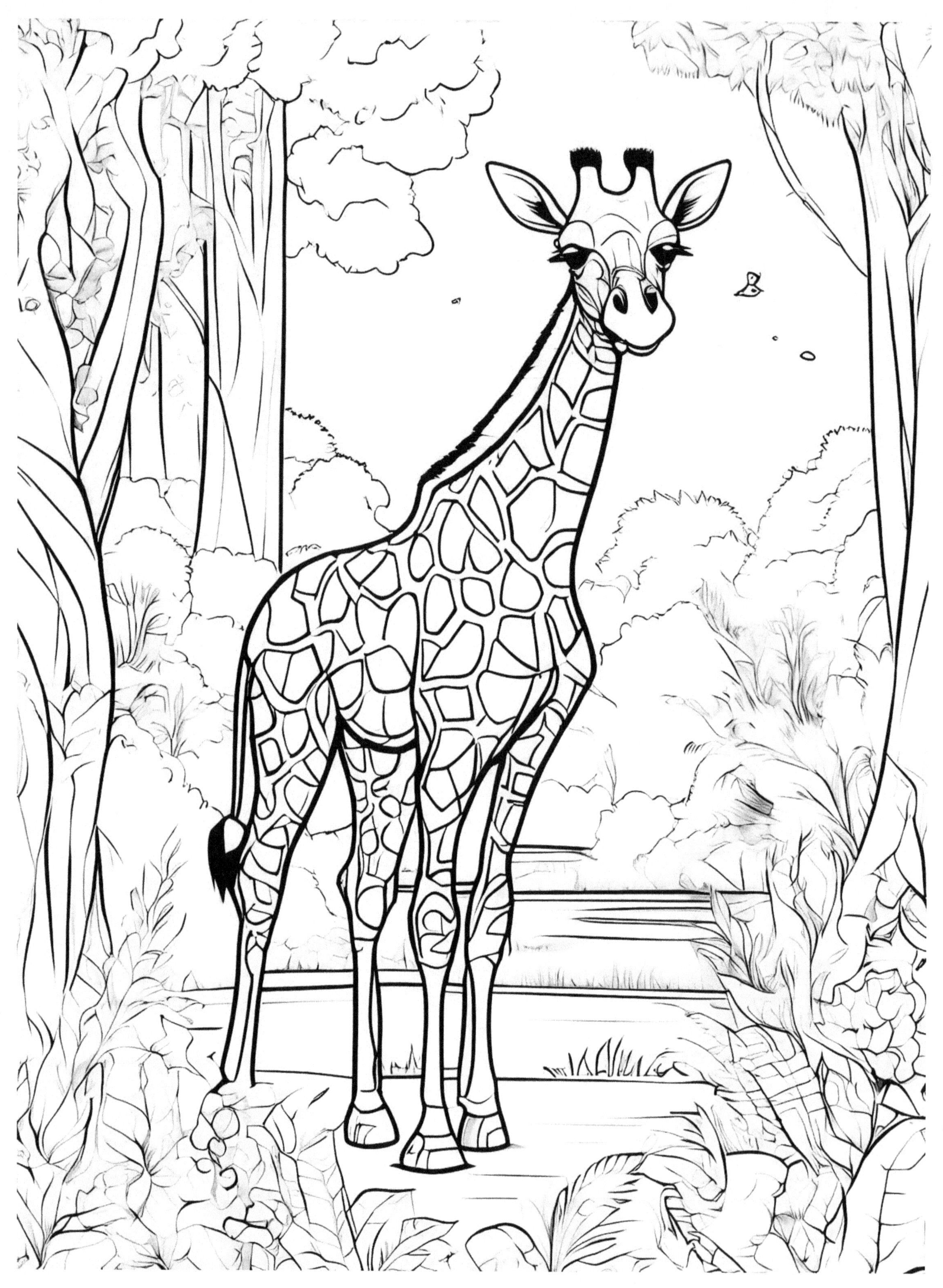

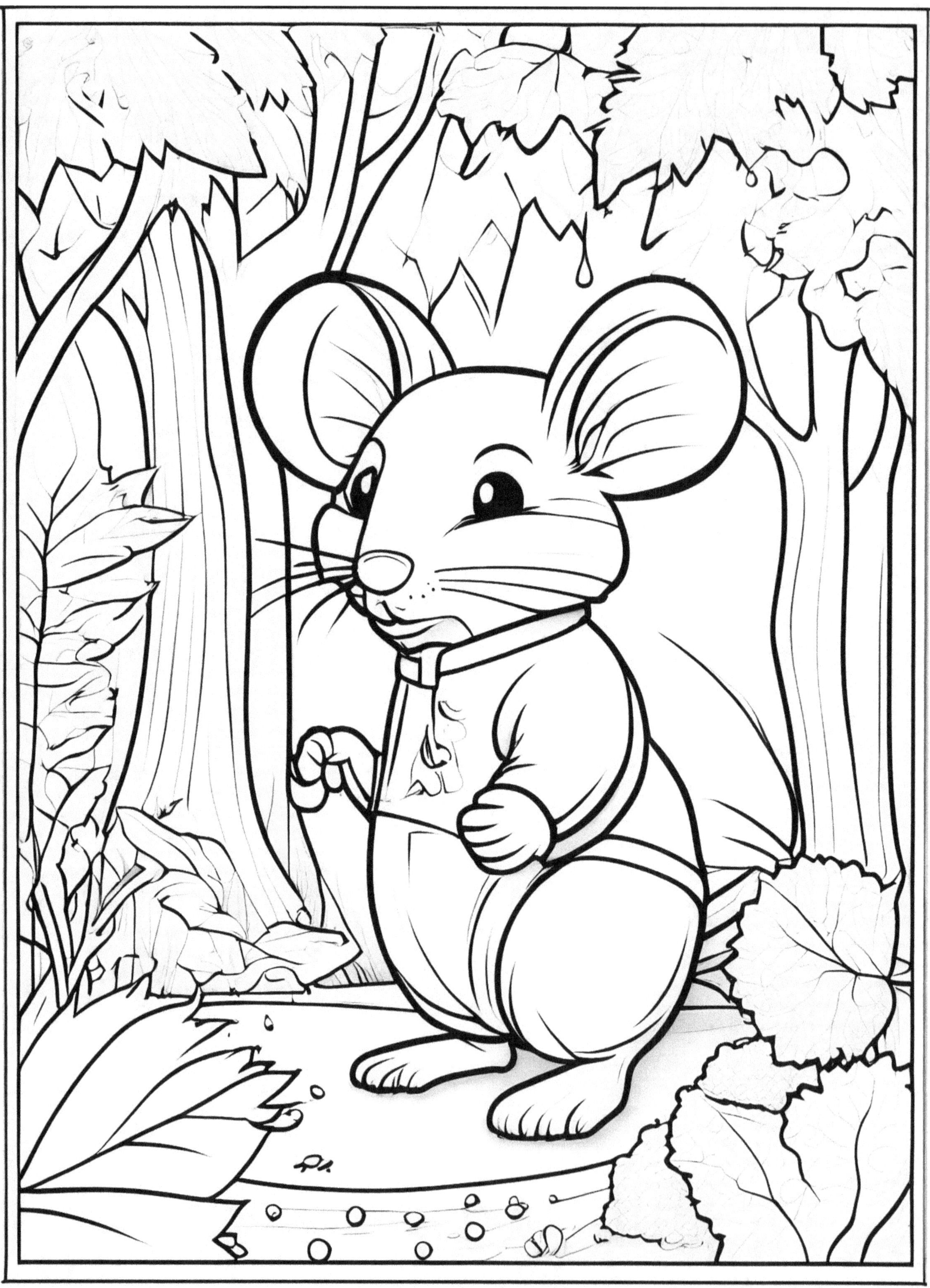

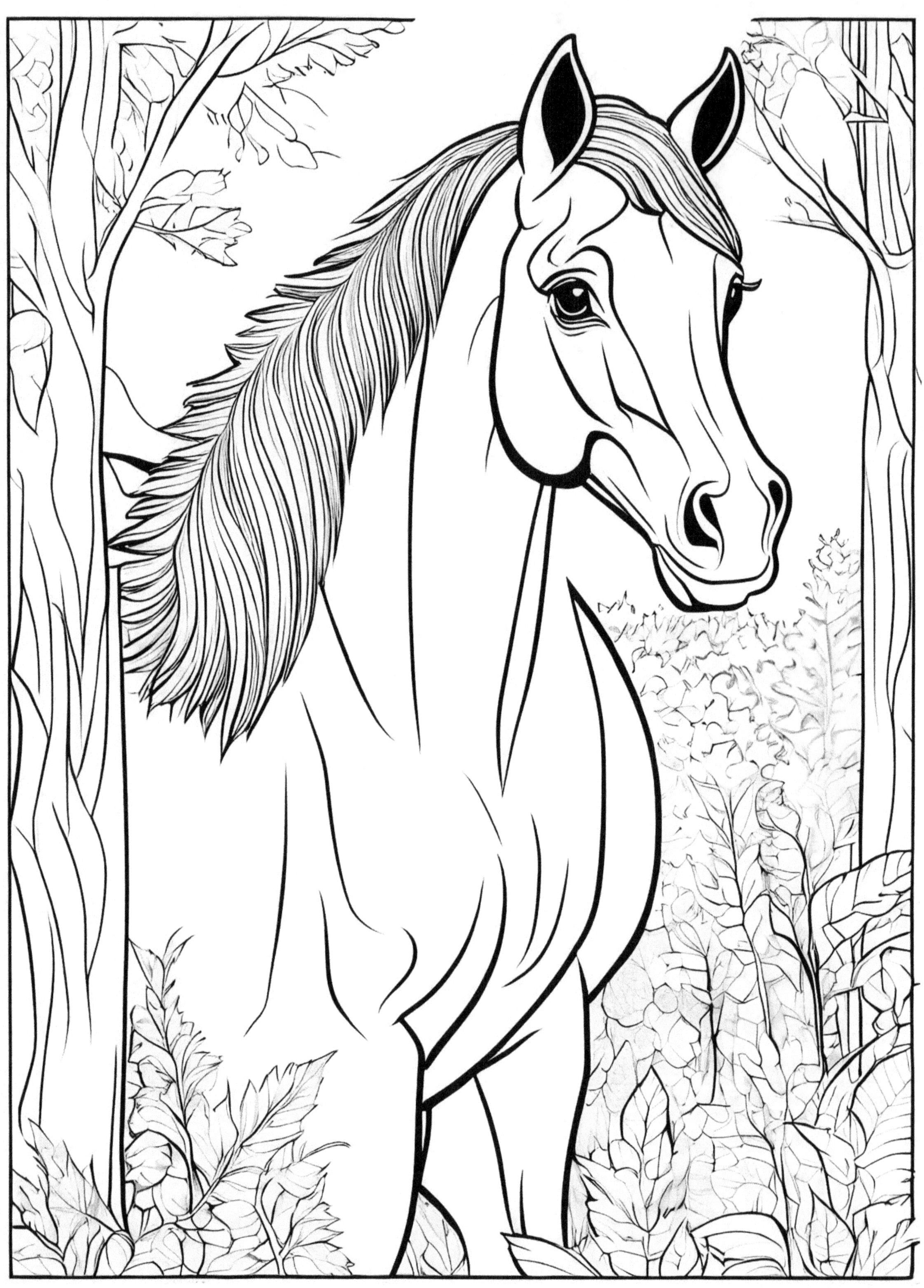

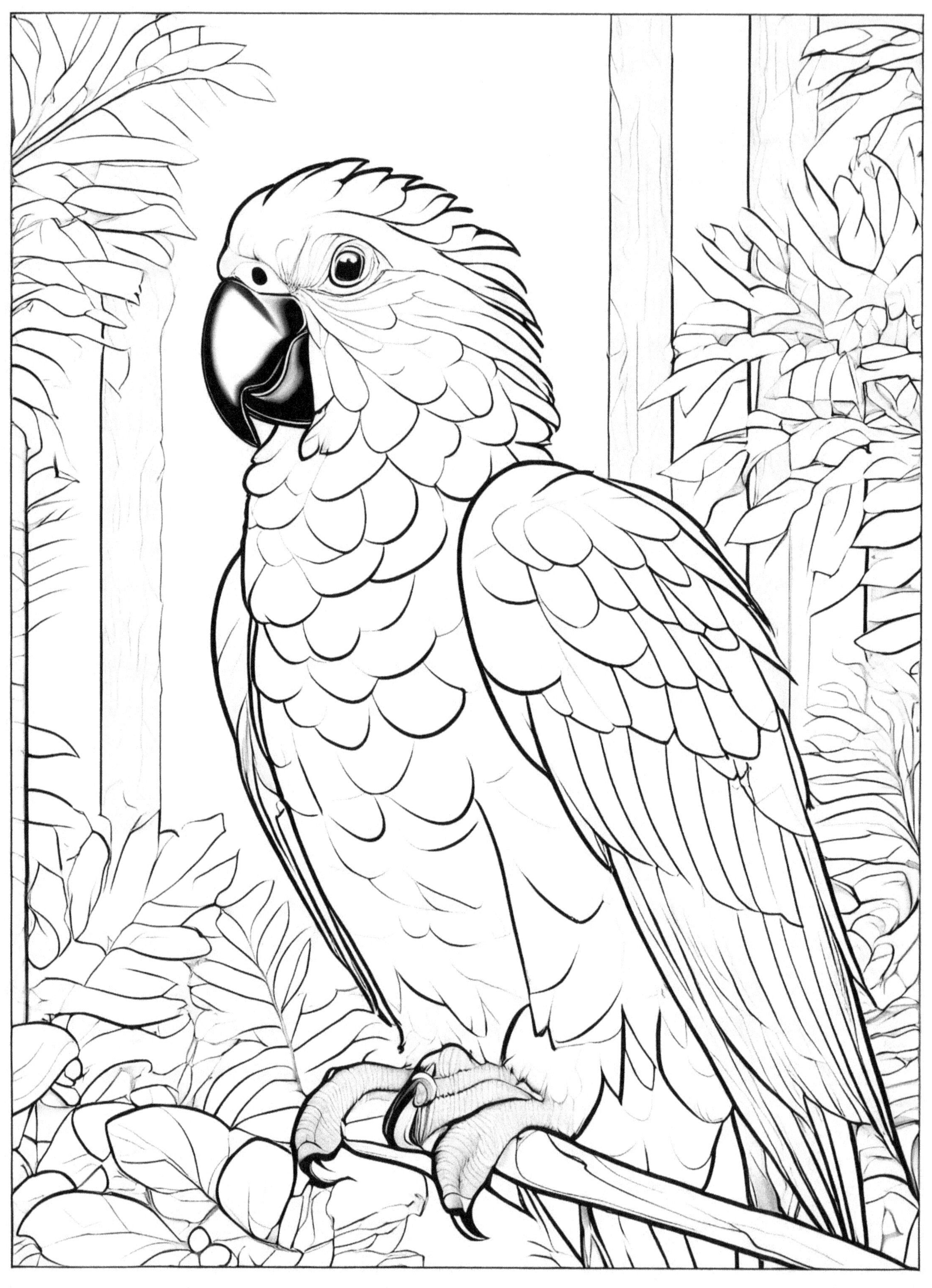

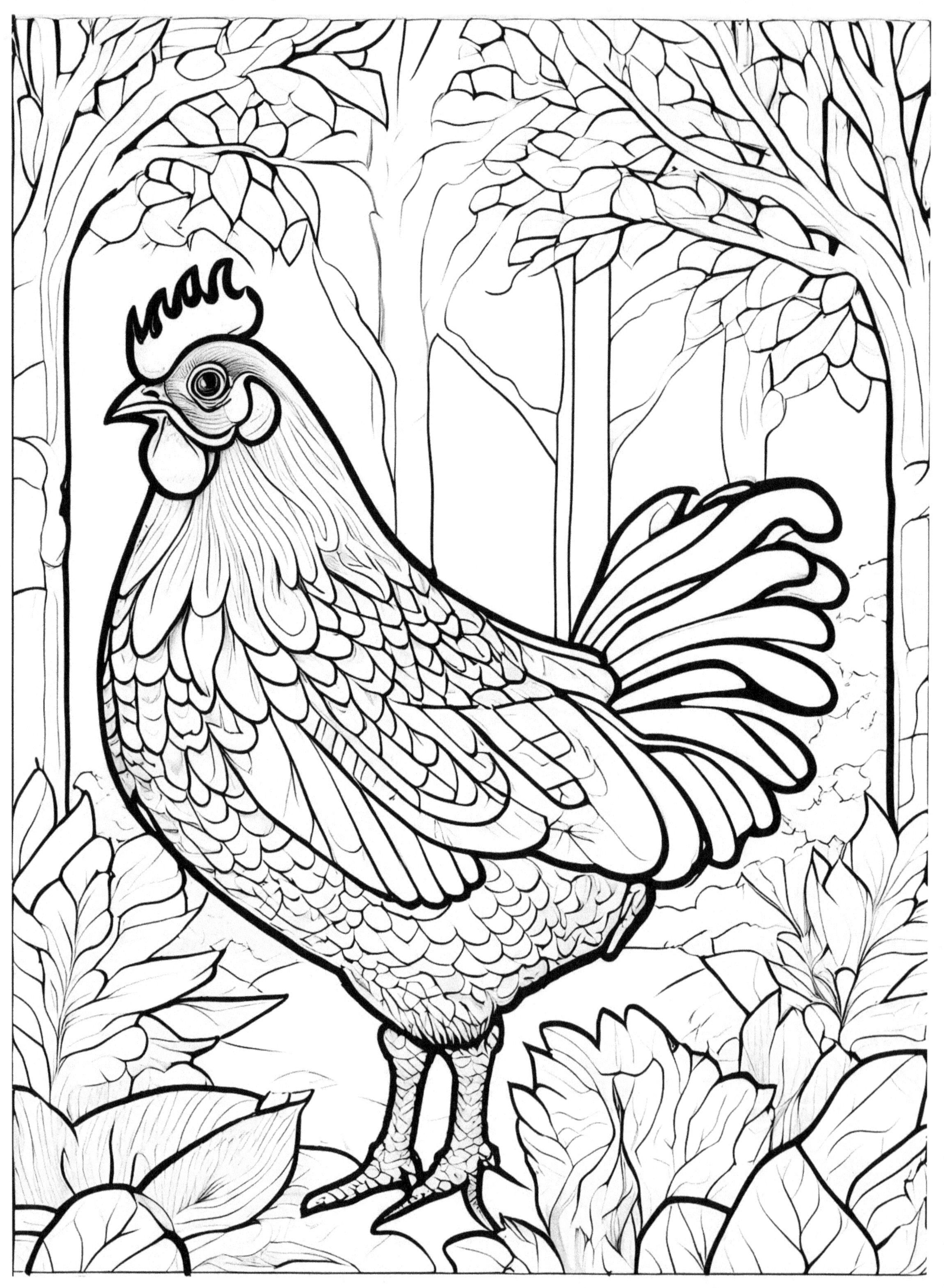

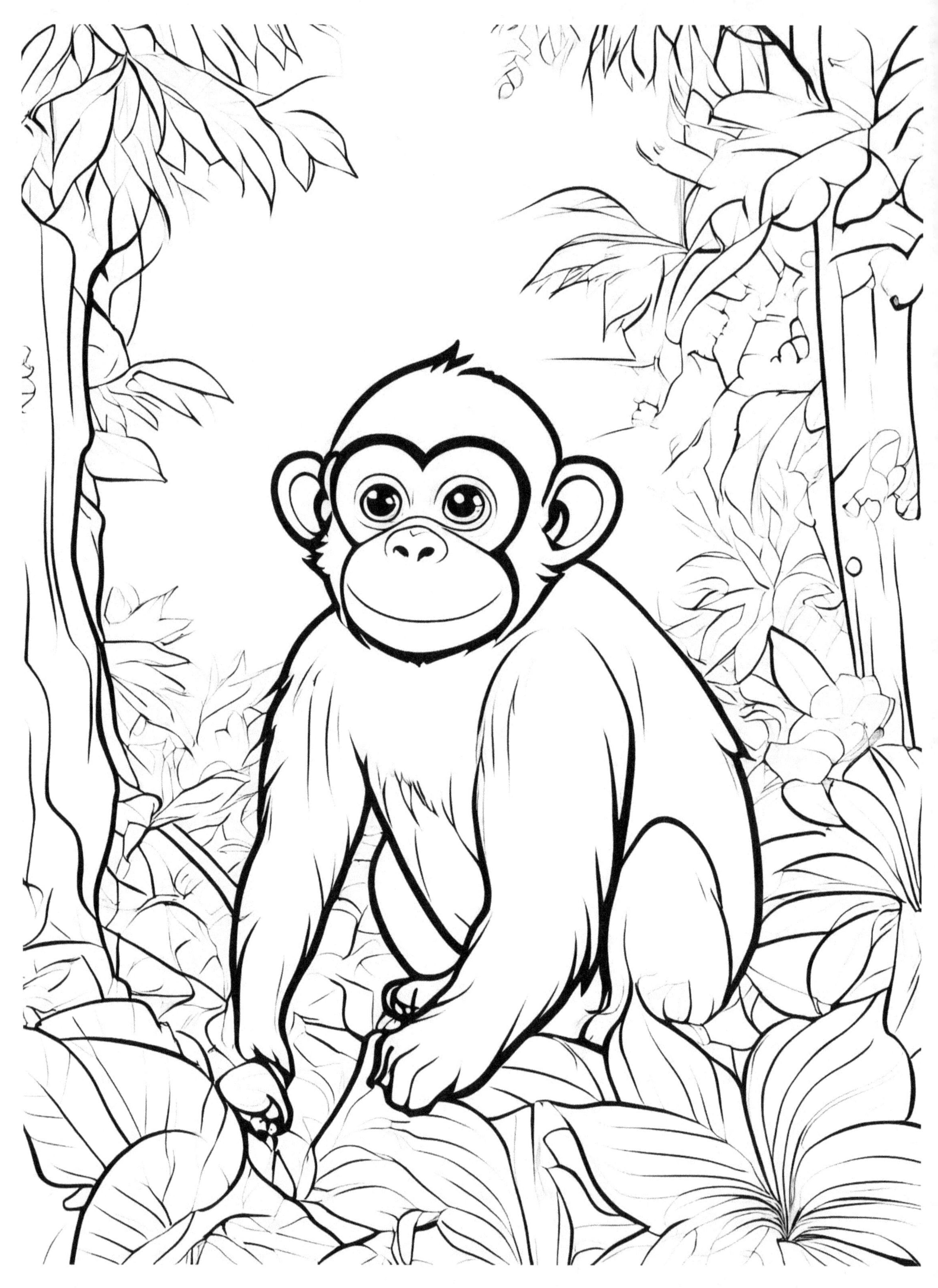

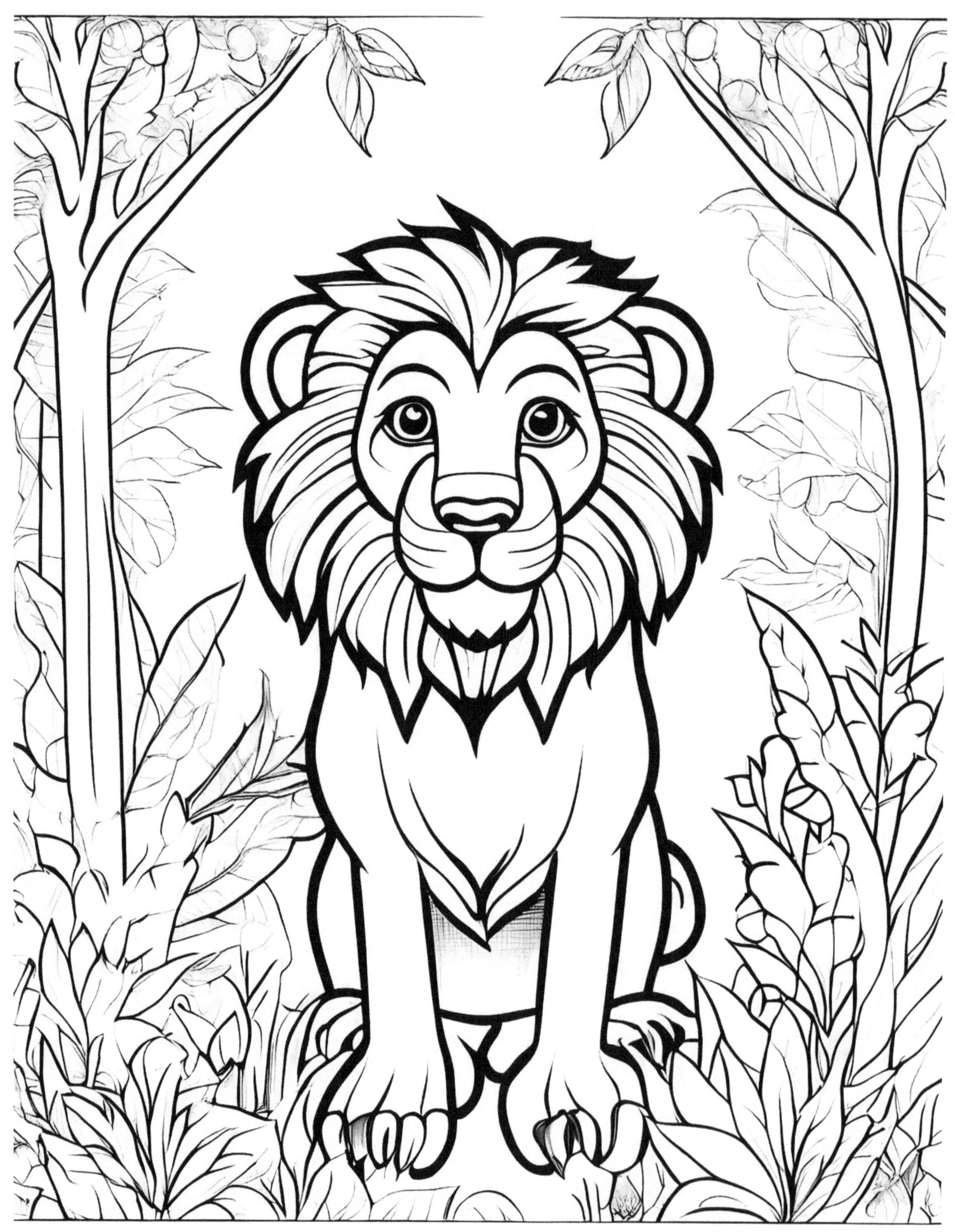

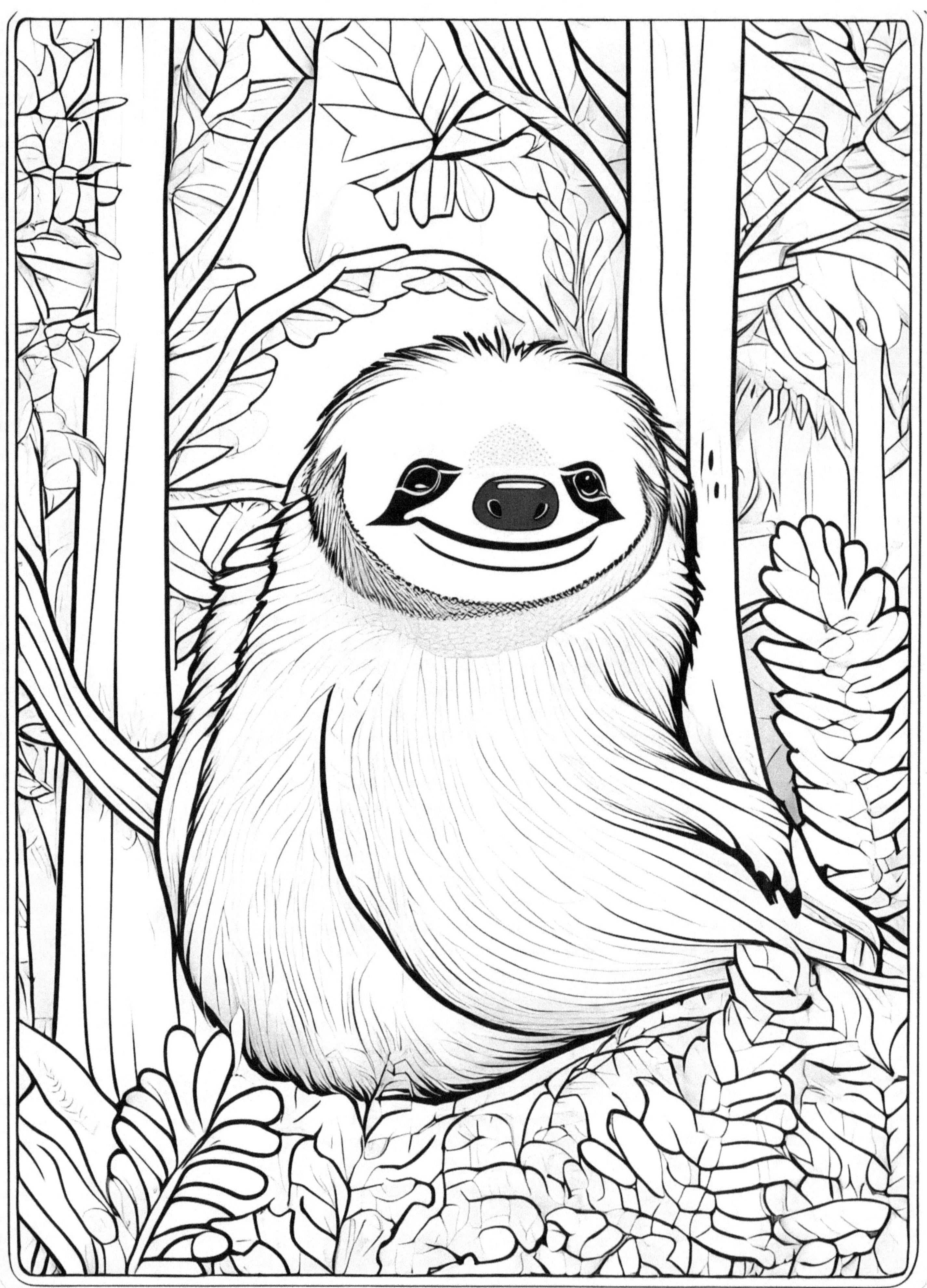

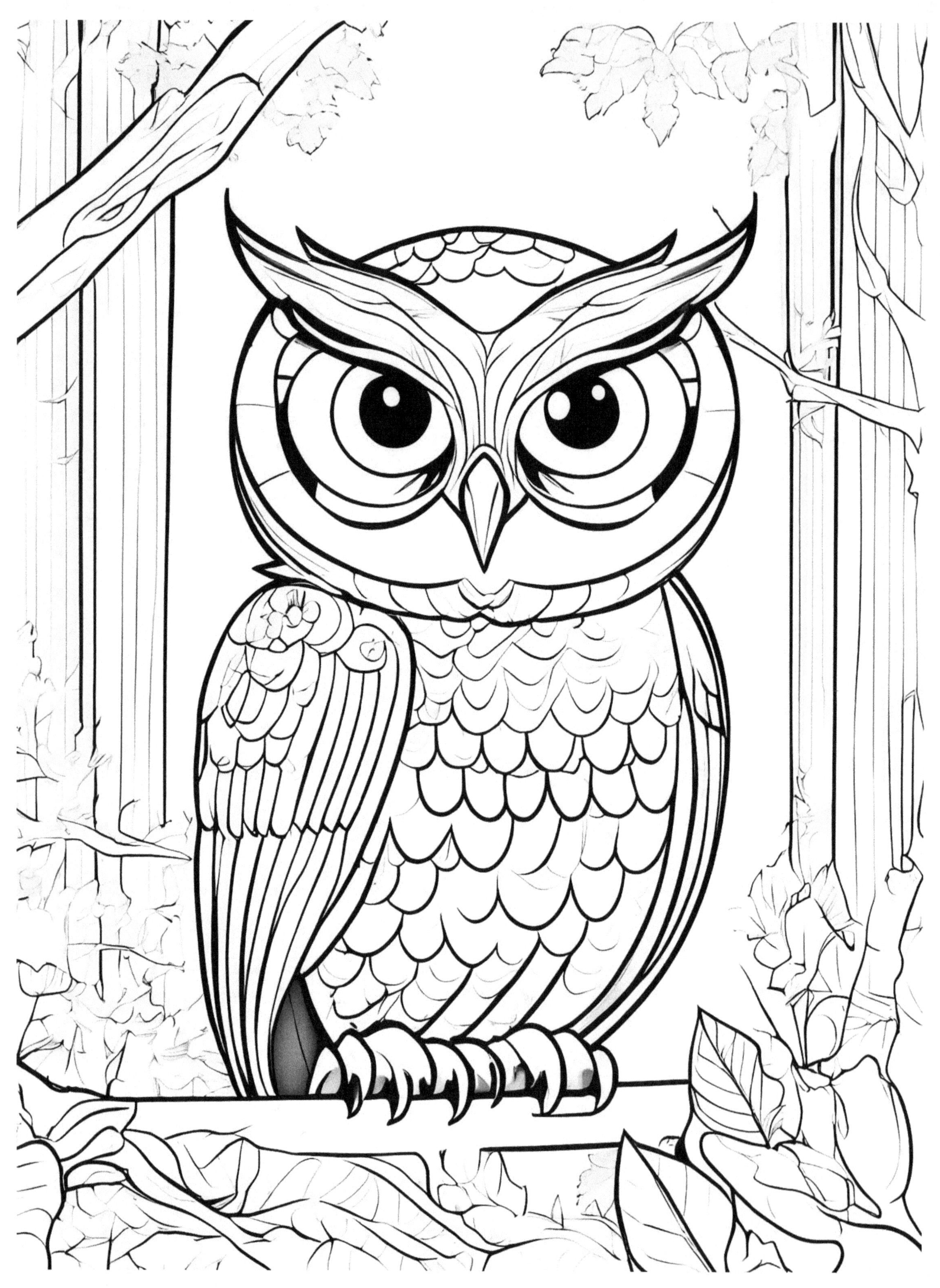

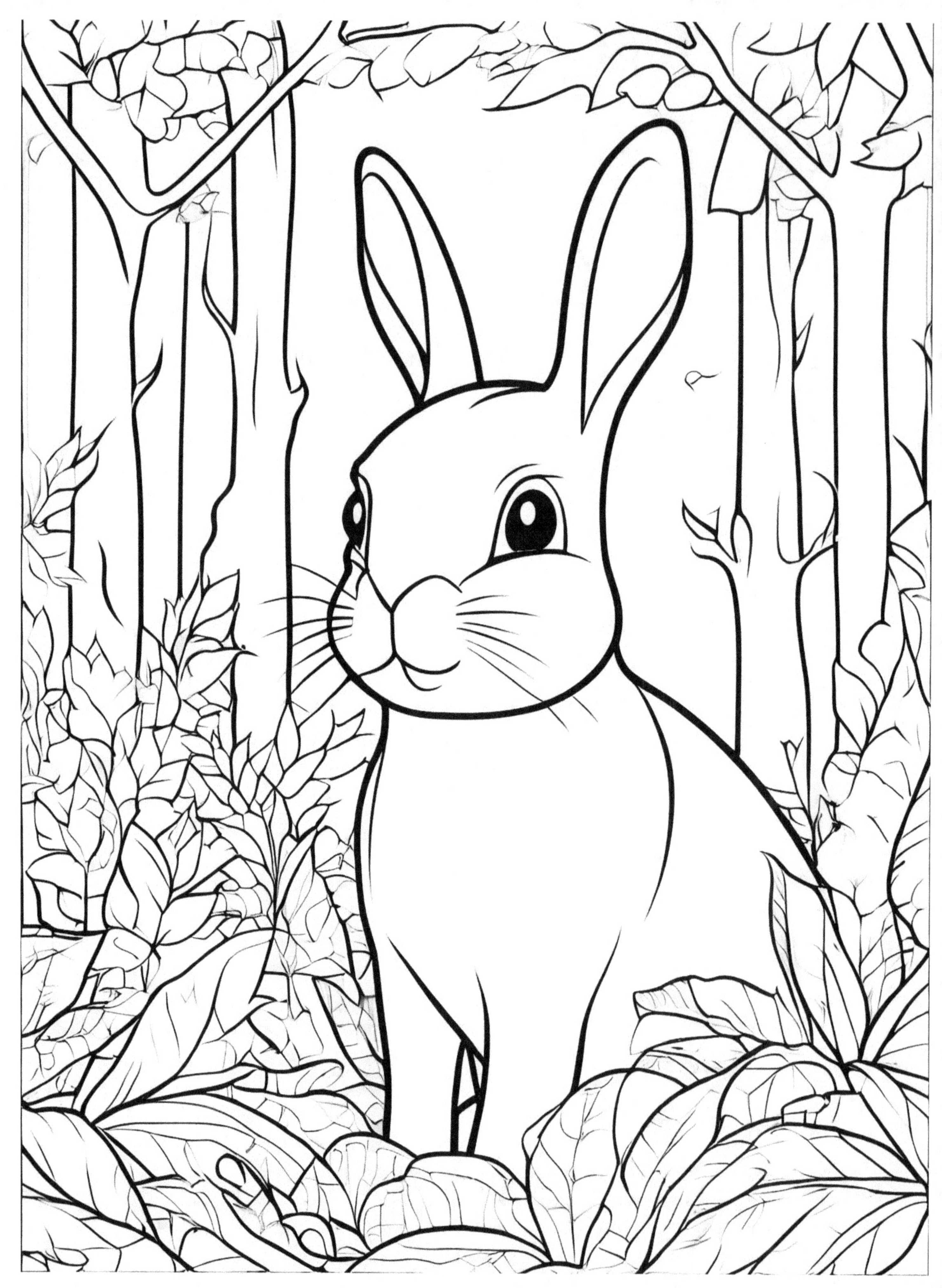

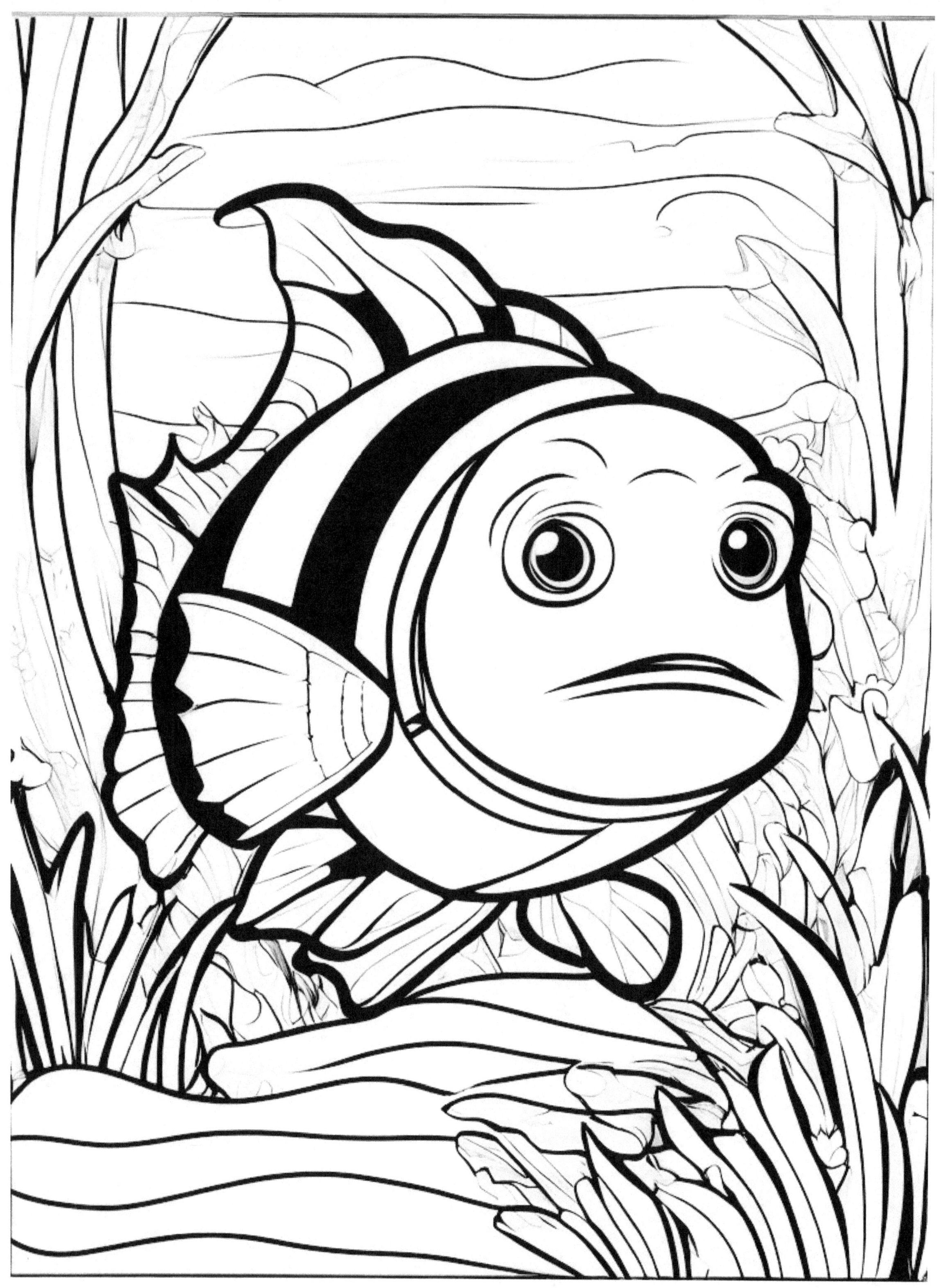

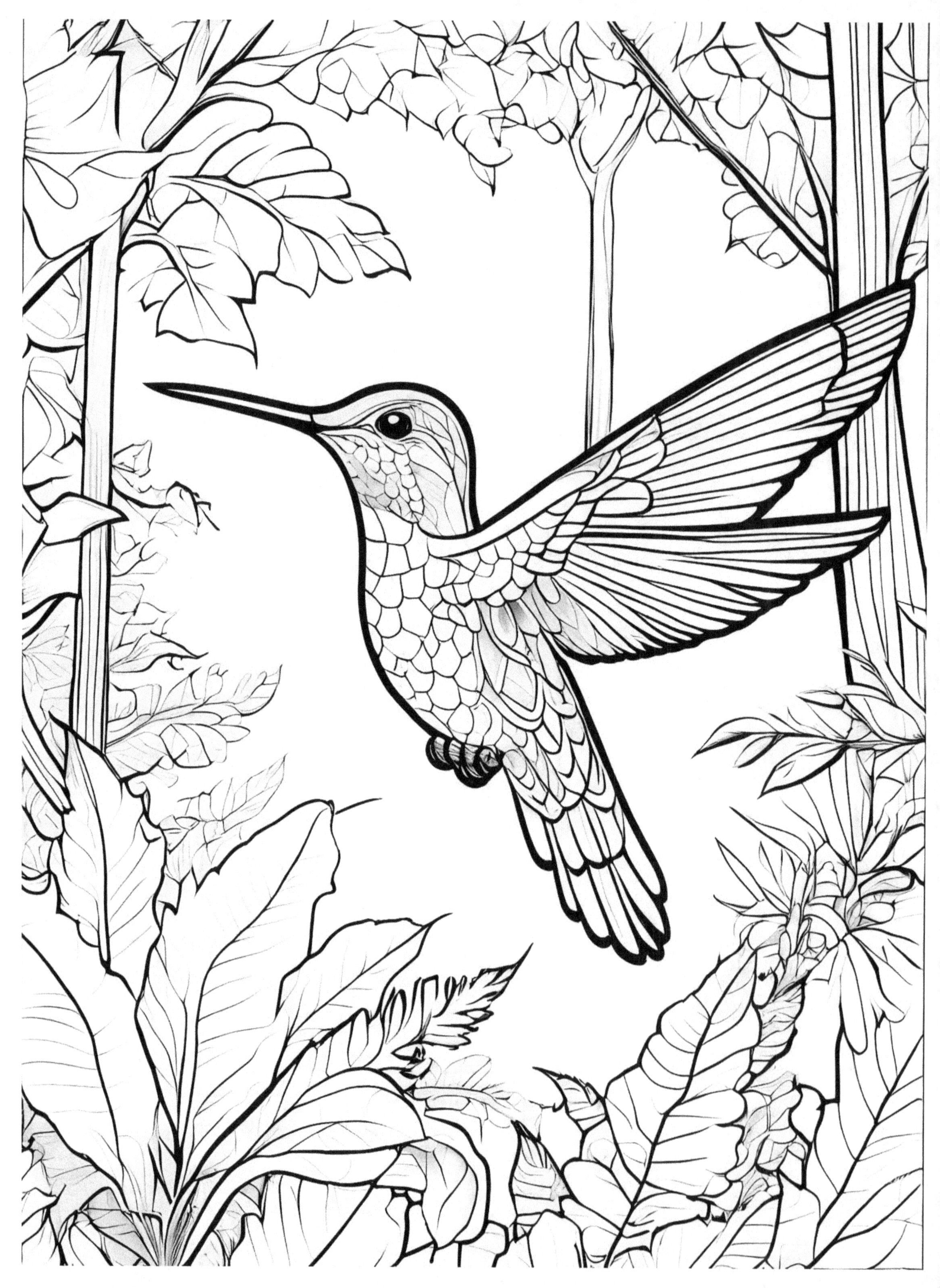

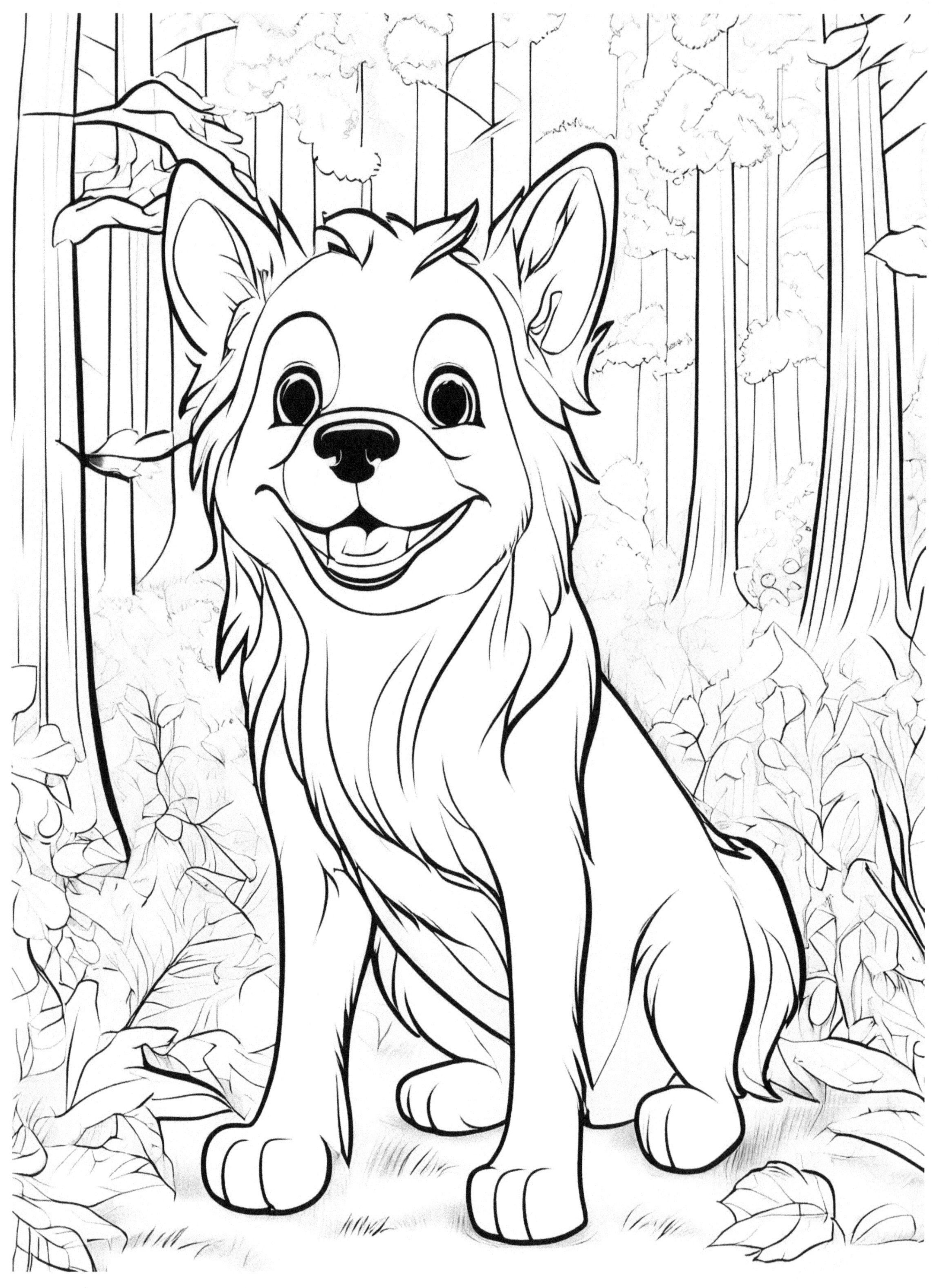

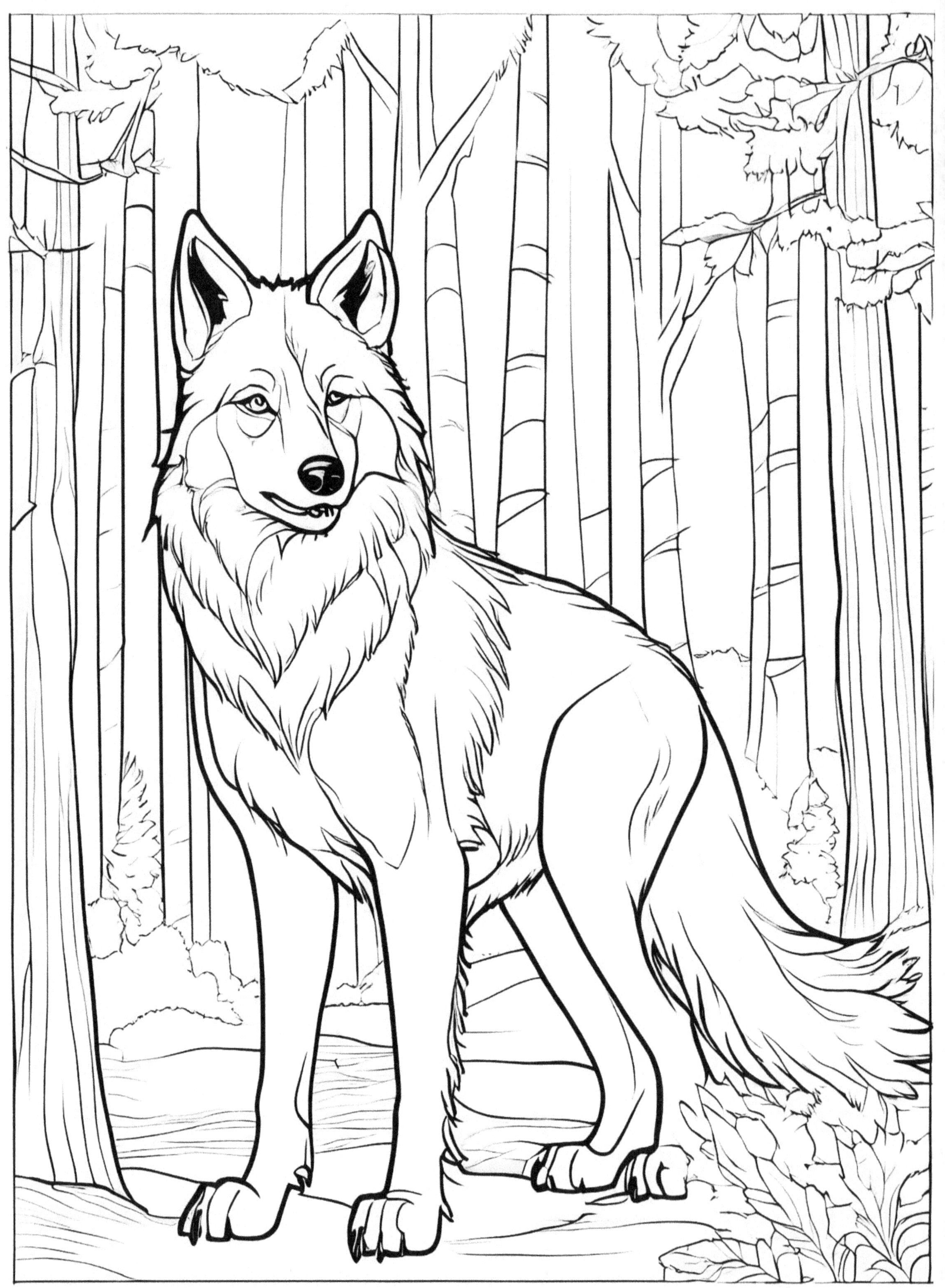